Holiday Gifts and Decorations Kids Can Make
(for Practically Nothing)

Written and illustrated by
Jerome C. Brown

Fearon Teacher Aids
Belmont, California

Editorial director: Ina Tabibian
Editor: Deborah Akers
Managing editor: Emily Hutchinson
Production editor: Stephen A. Shankland
Design director: Eleanor Mennick
Cover designer: Colleen Forbes
Compositor: Pamela Cattich
Manufacturing director: Casimira Kostecki

ISBN 0–8224–3595–9

Printed in the United States of America

1. 9 8 7

Contents

Picture Holders

Decorations and Ornaments

Introduction

Holiday Gifts and Decorations Kids Can Make (for Practically Nothing) contains 107 pages of reproducible activity sheets featuring gift and decoration projects that are fun, easy, and inexpensive to make. Each activity provides full instructions and diagrams, but younger children will undoubtedly require additional help and demonstration. Patterns are provided for many of the projects, though you should feel free to adapt or change any design to fit your group's needs and desires.

Construction paper is used in most of the projects in this book. It is referred to as art paper in the list of materials that accompanies each activity. You may also want to try using wallpaper samples, Con-Tact paper, newspaper, colorful magazine ads, or bright scraps of gift wrap. Any weight paper can be used. However, a heavier paper is more desirable for durability. Colors of art paper have been suggested, but these suggestions do not have to be followed.

Before you begin each project, always assemble the following items:

- White glue
- Pencil and eraser
- Scissors
- Crayons or colored felt pens
- Black felt pen

You will be using these materials for virtually every project in this book.

Here is a list of some basic items commonly found around the home that you might wish to collect and store for the projects in this book:

- Paper towel rolls
- Facial tissue boxes
- Cereal, oatmeal, and detergent boxes
- Shoe boxes
- Milk cartons (half-gallon size)
- Cardboard ice-cream containers
- Juice, fruit, tuna, and soup cans
- Glass bottles
- Plastic bottles
- Coffee cans (two-pound size)
- Yogurt container lids
- Mason jar lids
- Styrofoam egg cartons
- Clothespins
- Yarn
- Pipe cleaners
- Wire hangers
- Paper plates
- Red bricks
- Grocery sacks
- Old greeting cards

Here are some suggestions for managing paper and other materials for successful results:

Multiple Cutting. Cutting two or more pieces of paper at once is a timesaving technique. Generally, even blunt scissors are able to cut two pieces of paper at a time. However, never try to cut more than the scissors will cut easily.

Curling and Shaping. Flat stiff paper needs a little help to curl and bend. You can use one of several curling techniques: (1) Roll small pieces of paper, such as those used for hair, around a pencil; (2) Roll larger pieces of paper over the edge of a table or desk; (3) Pull the paper between your thumb and a closed pair of scissors.

Glue, Paste, and Stapler. Another important ingredient in creating with paper is a good glue or paste. White liquid glue is suggested in the materials lists because it really holds fast. But because white liquid glue runs and because it dries slowly, you may wish to have younger children use library paste. There are several brands available. When pasting, put paste on both pieces to be connected and then stick the pieces together. Certain projects, such as attaching notepaper to a notepad, require a stapler.

Coloring Materials. There are various materials and methods for children to use in coloring their designs: (1) When children are using crayons, have them place a few sheets of newspaper underneath the paper they are about to color for better results; (2) Colored felt pens are appropriate for many of these projects because of the bright colors available; (3) Allow children to use watercolors only if they have had some previous experience handling this medium or if you supervise closely; (4) Colored chalk can be used for shading. When it is necessary to brighten the cheeks of a face, apply some red chalk to the index finger and rub it on the cheek area. The projects that use chalk should be sprayed with a fixative such as hair spray to keep the chalk from rubbing off. An adult should always dispense this. Outdoors is the best place to use any spray to avoid having children inhale fumes.

Symmetrical Figures. The easiest way to achieve symmetry in cutouts is to fold the paper in half and draw or trace half the figure along the fold.

Supplies and Equipment. Reliable, proven materials and dependable tools make for successful art projects. If you are purchasing your own equipment and supplies, look for reliable brand names and choose carefully.

Walnut Shell Creatures

Materials

1/2 walnut shell
3″ × 3″ black art paper
    (backing)
Art paper of various colors
Plastic eyes (optional)
Pipe cleaner (reindeer)
Safety pin
Shellac (optional)
Tempera paint and brush
    (optional)
Cotton balls (Santa)

Procedure

For Santa and reindeer:

1. Shellac or paint walnut shell if you desire.
2. Glue walnut shell to black paper (fig. A).
3. When glue is dry, trim off excess black paper.
4. Use art-paper scraps to make details. Glue on plastic or art-paper eyes.
5. For reindeer, make antlers with pipe cleaner and glue in place. For Santa, cut up cotton balls and make beard and trim. Glue in place.
6. Tape safety pin in place (fig. B).

For owl:

1. Follow procedures 2 and 3 above. Do not shellac or paint shell.
2. Cut wings and horns from brown art paper and glue in place.
3. Cut beak from yellow paper and glue in place.
4. Glue plastic or art-paper eyes in place.
5. Draw chest feathers and feet with felt pen.
6. Tape safety pin in place (fig. B).

Figure A

Figure B

2

Designer Sunglasses Holder

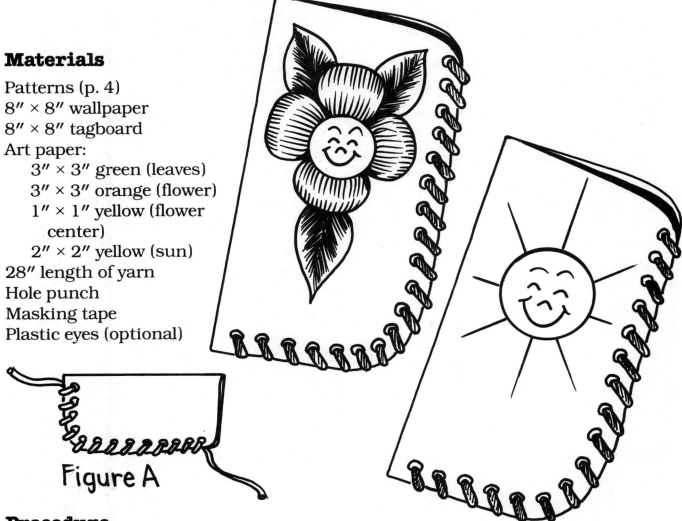

Materials

Patterns (p. 4)
8″ × 8″ wallpaper
8″ × 8″ tagboard
Art paper:
    3″ × 3″ green (leaves)
    3″ × 3″ orange (flower)
    1″ × 1″ yellow (flower center)
    2″ × 2″ yellow (sun)
28″ length of yarn
Hole punch
Masking tape
Plastic eyes (optional)

Figure A

Procedure

1. Trace holder pattern on wallpaper with black felt pen.
2. Glue wallpaper to tagboard. Allow to dry, then cut along lines.
3. Place pattern on cutout and punch out holes where indicated.
4. Fold holder in half carefully, lining up the holes. Do not crease the folded edge.
5. For more effective threading, wrap a piece of tape around one inch of one end of the yarn. Tie a knot at the other end, leaving two inches of yarn from knot for tying when finished.
6. Start threading (fig. A), using the stitch shown. Stitch through the last hole. Tie knot. Trim excess yarn.
7. Cut out sun face or flower and leaves from art paper and glue in place on holder.
8. Draw details with felt pen.

3

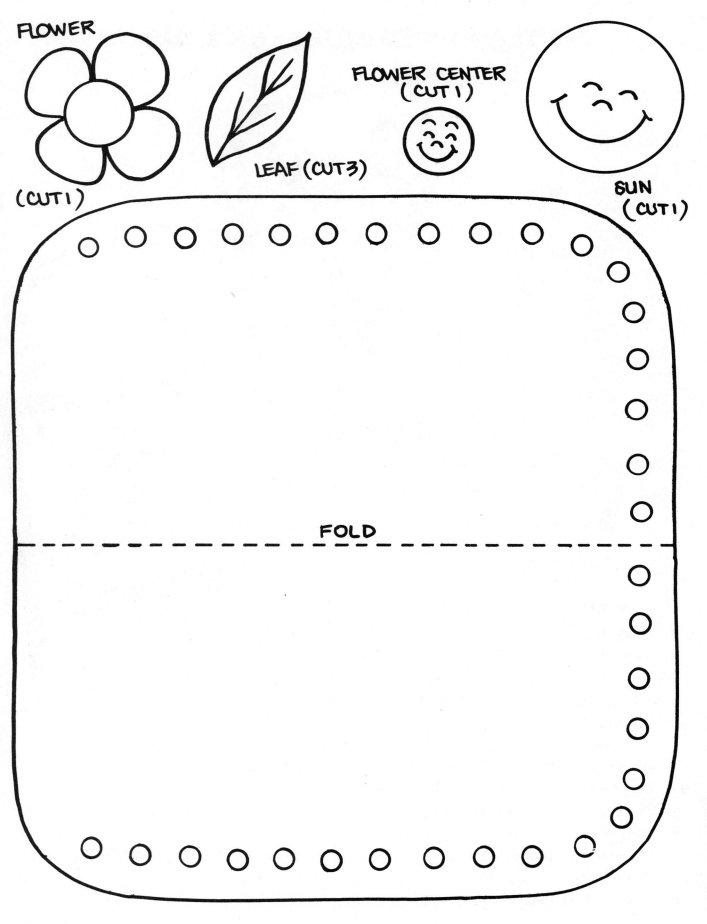

FLOWER

(CUT1)

LEAF (CUT3)

FLOWER CENTER
(CUT 1)

SUN
(CUT1)

FOLD

Holiday Gifts and Decorations, © 1986

Tiger or Owl Book Cover

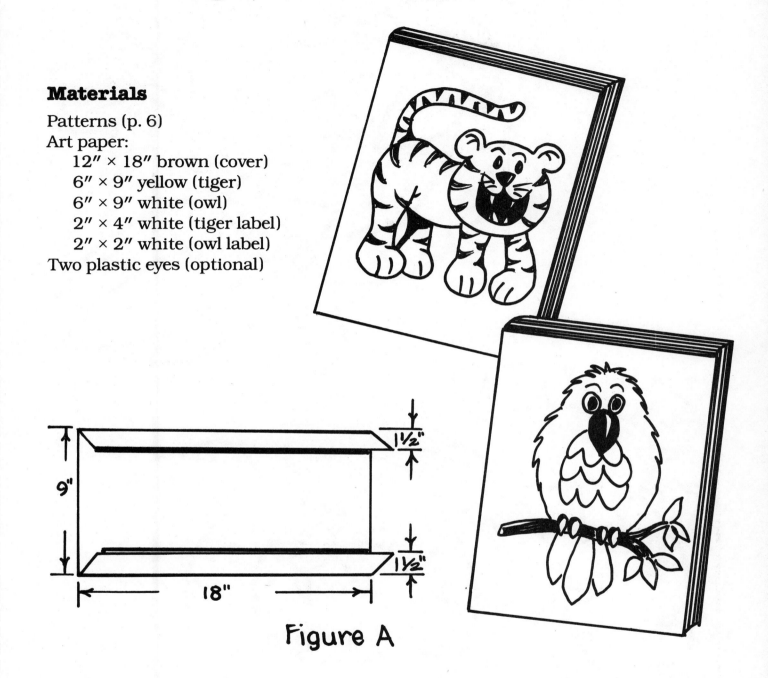

Materials

Patterns (p. 6)
Art paper:
    12″ × 18″ brown (cover)
    6″ × 9″ yellow (tiger)
    6″ × 9″ white (owl)
    2″ × 4″ white (tiger label)
    2″ × 2″ white (owl label)
Two plastic eyes (optional)

Figure A

Procedure

1. Make a 1½″ fold along both long edges of brown paper (fig. A). This will make a 9″-wide book cover.
2. Trace chosen pattern on art paper with black felt pen. Color, cut out, and glue to front of cover.
3. Glue plastic eyes in place or draw eyes with felt pen.
4. Print letters with felt pen on white label. Glue in place.

Holiday Gifts and Decorations, © 1986

6 *Tiger or Owl Book Cover*

Egg Carton Necklace or Bracelet

Materials

Styrofoam egg cartons of
  various colors
Hole punch
Needle and thread or fishing
  line
Small beads

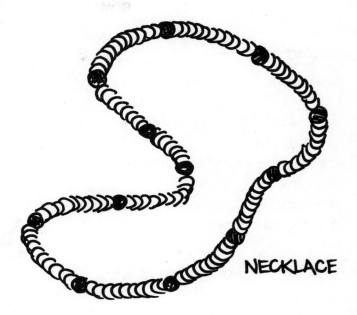

NECKLACE

BRACELET

Procedure

1. Punch out a sufficient number of styrofoam discs from egg cartons.
2. String 15 discs together with needle and thread. Add a bead.
3. Repeat this process until necklace or bracelet is desired length.
4. Tie ends of thread or fishing line together securely.

Tuna Can Coin or Jewelry Holder

Materials

6½-ounce tuna can

1½″ × 12″ wallpaper that resembles shirt or blouse material

Art-paper scraps of various colors

20″ length of yarn

Small paper doily

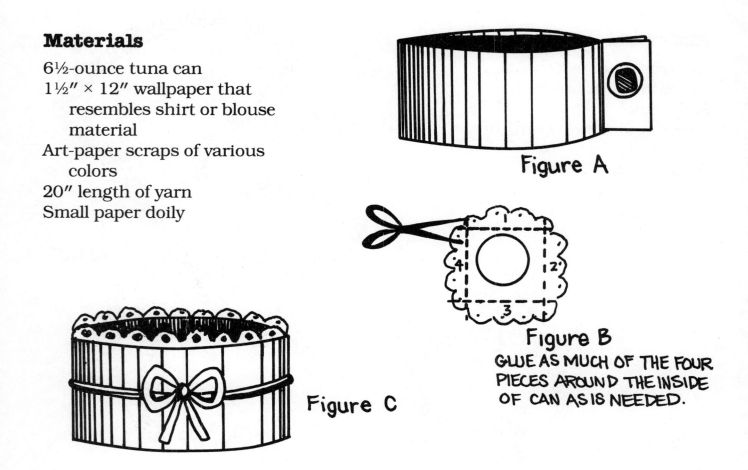

Figure A

Figure B

GLUE AS MUCH OF THE FOUR PIECES AROUND THE INSIDE OF CAN AS IS NEEDED.

Figure C

Procedure

For coin holder:

1. Wrap wallpaper strip around can and glue in place. If decorating can with bow tie, overlap edges of wallpaper and glue. If making a French cuff and cuff link, extend ends of wallpaper as shown, then glue together (fig. A).
2. Cut bow tie or cuff link from art paper and glue in place.

For jewelry holder:

1. Wrap wallpaper strip around can and glue in place.
2. Cut doily as shown (fig. B). Glue outer edge to inside of can (fig. C).
3. Glue yarn in place and tie it in a bow (fig. C).

Holiday Gifts and Decorations, © 1986

Paper Roll Napkin Rings

Materials

Patterns (p. 10)

Three bathroom paper rolls

Art paper:

    six 2¼″ × 5½″ of any color (rolls)

    two 9″ × 12″ of any color (figures)

Six 19″ lengths of yarn

X-acto knife

Procedure

1. With X-acto knife, cut each paper roll in half to make six napkin rings.
2. Glue one 2¼″ × 5½″ paper strip around each ring.
3. Tie a yarn bow around each ring, leaving three-inch ends. Glue yarn in place.
4. Trace each pattern twice on any color of art paper. Color and add details with crayons or felt pens and then cut out. To each ring, glue a matching pair of cutouts, one to each end of yarn bow.

Holiday Gifts and Decorations, © 1986

Holiday Gifts and Decorations, © 1986

Soap Box Recipe Holder

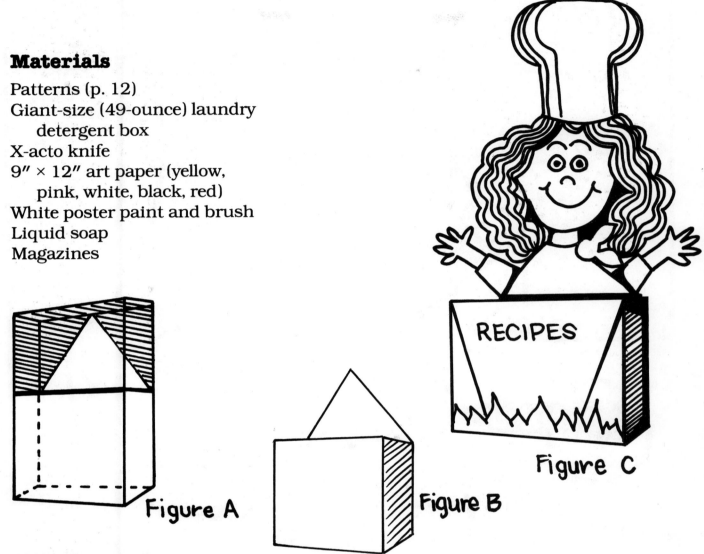

Materials

Patterns (p. 12)
Giant-size (49-ounce) laundry
  detergent box
X-acto knife
9″ × 12″ art paper (yellow,
  pink, white, black, red)
White poster paint and brush
Liquid soap
Magazines

Figure A

Figure B

RECIPES

Figure C

Procedure

1. With X-acto knife, cut box as shown (figs. A and B).
2. Add one teaspoon of liquid soap to poster paint. (The soap helps paint adhere to box.)
3. Paint box. Allow to dry.
4. Draw pot on black paper and flames on red paper. Cut out and glue to front of painted box (fig. C).
5. Trace patterns on art paper and cut out.
6. Assemble and glue all cutouts as shown.
7. Draw facial details with felt pen.
8. Cut out and then glue on letters from magazines to spell the word *Recipes*.

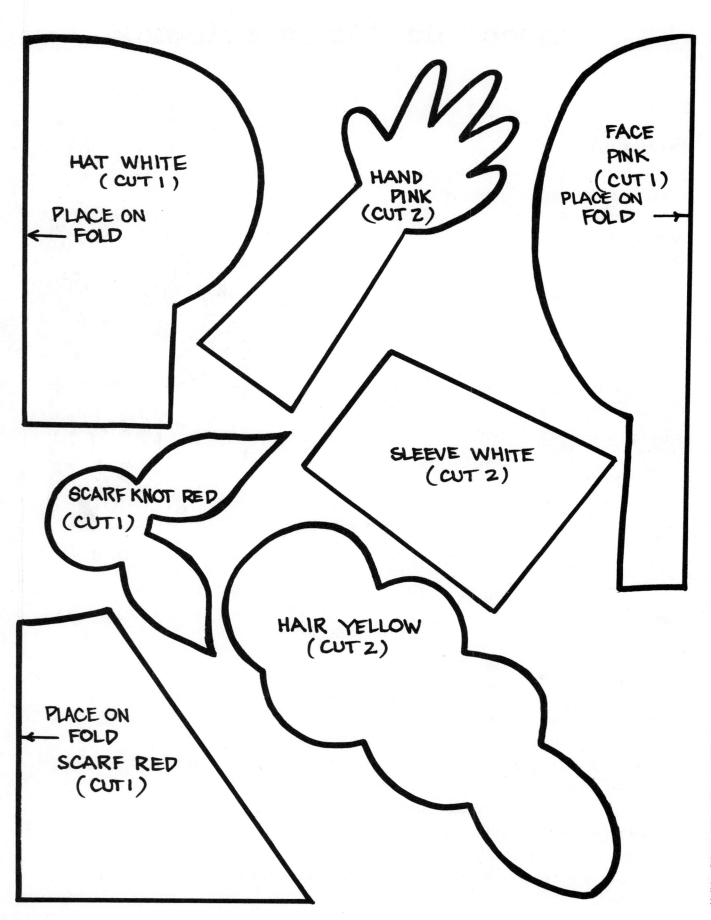

HAT WHITE
(CUT 1)

PLACE ON
← FOLD

HAND
PINK
(CUT 2)

FACE
PINK
(CUT 1)
PLACE ON
FOLD →

SLEEVE WHITE
(CUT 2)

SCARF KNOT RED
(CUT 1)

HAIR YELLOW
(CUT 2)

PLACE ON
← FOLD
SCARF RED
(CUT 1)

Holiday Gifts and Decorations, © 1986

Tissue Box Coupon Holder

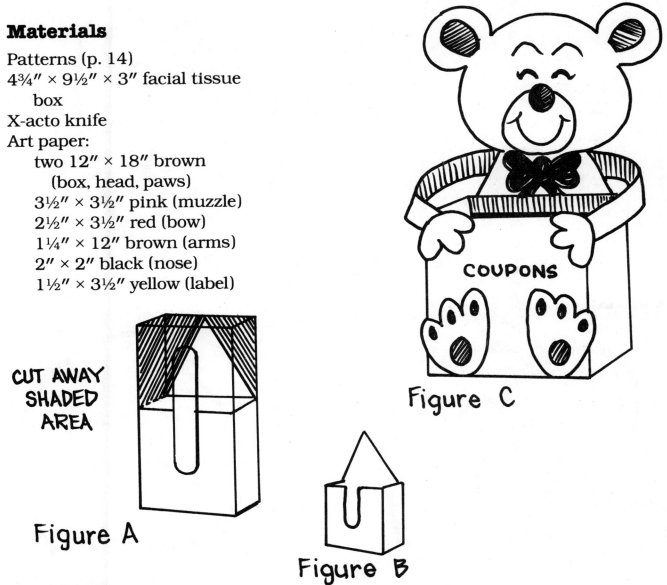

Materials

Patterns (p. 14)
4¾″ × 9½″ × 3″ facial tissue
    box
X-acto knife
Art paper:
    two 12″ × 18″ brown
      (box, head, paws)
    3½″ × 3½″ pink (muzzle)
    2½″ × 3½″ red (bow)
    1¼″ × 12″ brown (arms)
    2″ × 2″ black (nose)
    1½″ × 3½″ yellow (label)

CUT AWAY
SHADED
AREA

Figure A

Figure B

COUPONS

Figure C

Procedure

1. With X-acto knife, cut box as shown (figs. A and B).
2. Cover box with brown paper and glue in place.
3. Trace patterns on art paper and cut out. Cut two 1¼″ × 6″ strips of brown paper for arms.
4. Assemble and glue all cutouts as shown (fig. C).
5. Draw details on face and feet with black felt pen or crayon.
6. Print *Coupons* on yellow paper with felt pen or crayon. Glue to front of bear.

Holiday Gifts and Decorations, © 1986

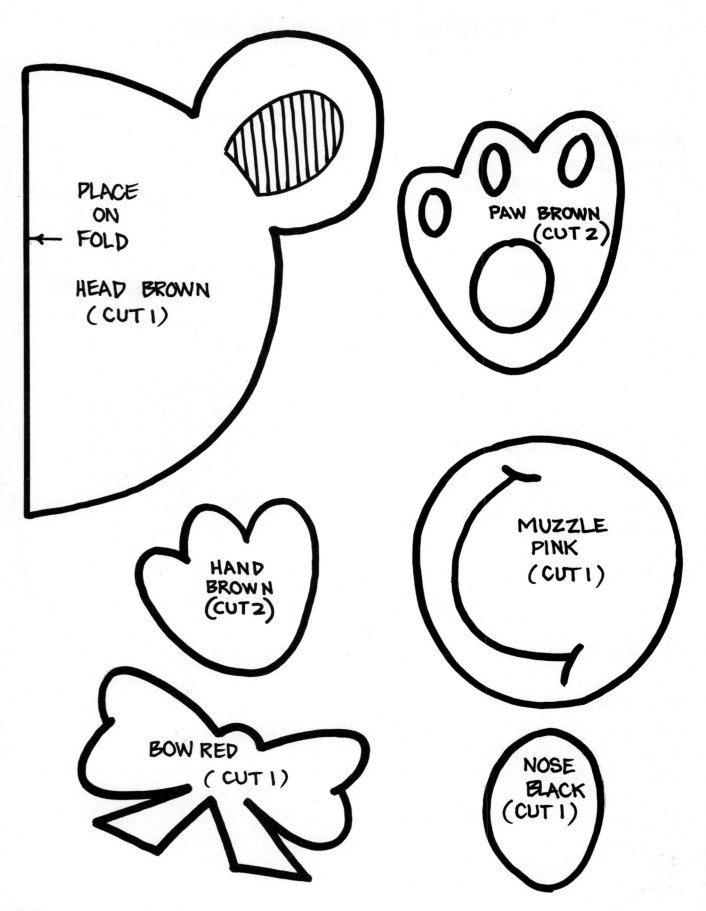

PLACE
ON
FOLD

HEAD BROWN
(CUT 1)

PAW BROWN
(CUT 2)

HAND
BROWN
(CUT 2)

MUZZLE
PINK
(CUT 1)

BOW RED
(CUT 1)

NOSE
BLACK
(CUT 1)

14 *Tissue Box Coupon Holder*

Tissue Box Mailbox

Materials

Patterns (p. 16)
4¾″ × 9½″ × 3″ facial tissue
box
X-acto knife
Art paper:
12″ × 18″ blue (box)
7″ × 6″ white (eagle)
2½″ × 9″ yellow (stars)
4″ × 6″ red (flag)
Hole punch
Brass fastener

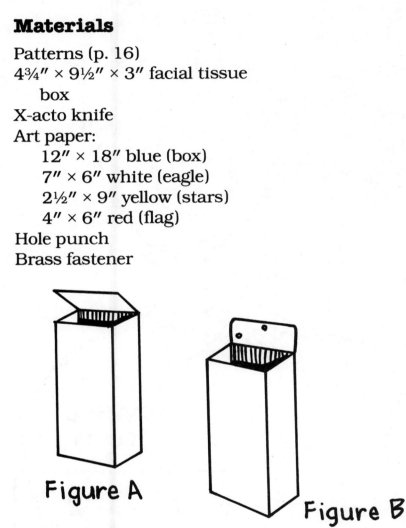

Figure A

Figure B

Procedure

1. With X-acto knife, cut one end of box to make flap (fig. A).
2. Cover outside and flap with blue paper. Glue in place.
3. Trace patterns on art paper and cut out.
4. Draw details on eagle and color with crayons or felt pens.
5. Glue eagle and stars on box as shown.
6. Print letters on flag with black felt pen. Punch two holes on flap—one
   to hang mailbox and the other to attach brass fastener and flag (fig. B).

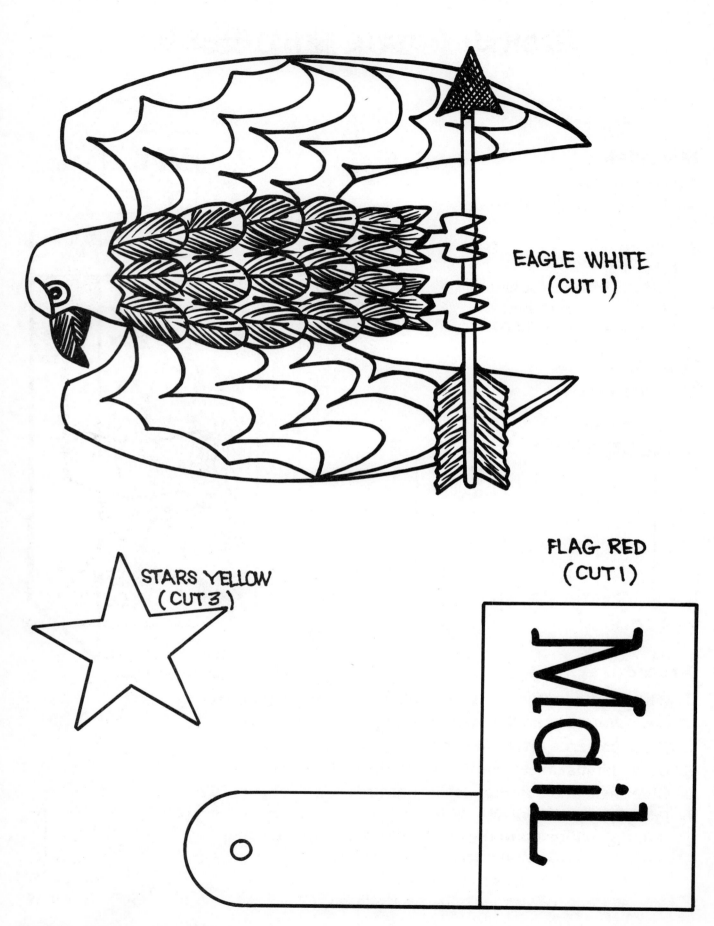

EAGLE WHITE
(CUT 1)

STARS YELLOW
(CUT 3)

FLAG RED
(CUT 1)

Mail

Bleach Bottle Coin Bank

Materials

Patterns (this page)
Plastic two-quart bleach
    container
Art paper:
    12″ × 18″ red (hat)
    1½″ × 18″ green (scarf)
    6″ × 8″ blue (earmuffs)
    scraps of green and red
      (holly and berries)
Stapler
Red chalk
Plastic eyes (optional)
Small red ornament (nose)
X-acto knife

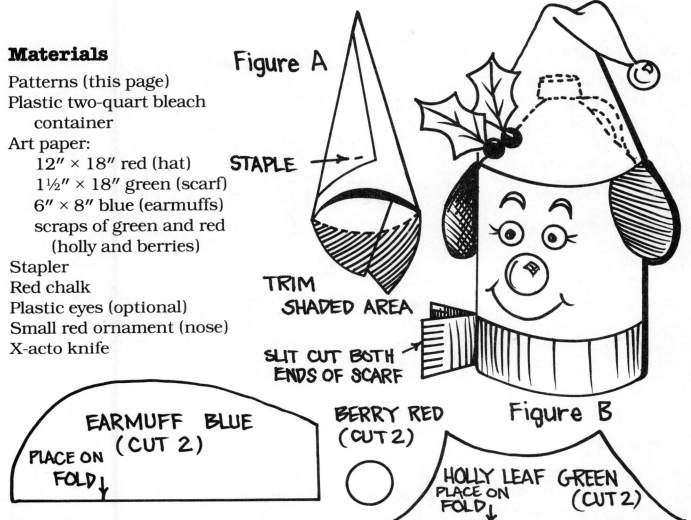

Figure A

STAPLE →

TRIM SHADED AREA

SLIT CUT BOTH ENDS OF SCARF

Figure B

EARMUFF BLUE (CUT 2)
PLACE ON FOLD ↓

BERRY RED (CUT 2)

HOLLY LEAF GREEN (CUT 2)
PLACE ON FOLD ↓

Figure C

REAR VIEW

Procedure

1. Make hat by rolling red paper into a cone. Staple, glue, and trim (fig. A).
   Bend top of hat. Push hat down over top of container and glue in place
   (fig. B).
2. Trace patterns and cut out.
3. Glue on earmuffs and scarf strip (fig. B).
4. Cut small X where nose will be placed. Put glue on ornament
   stem and push through X spot.
5. Glue plastic or art-paper eyes in place.
6. Draw eyebrows and mouth with felt pen.
7. Smudge red chalk on cheeks to add color.
8. Glue holly and berries to hat (fig. B).
9. Cut coin slot in back with X-acto knife (fig. C).

Holiday Gifts and Decorations, © 1986

Container Lid Stand-Up Picture

Materials

Greeting card or photo
Ice-cream lid
2″ × 2″ cardboard
Stapler
Poster paint and brush
Hair spray and glitter

Procedure

1. Paint lid and cardboard with poster paint. Allow to dry.
2. Trace lid on back of selected card or photo. Cut and trim card to fit circular lid. Glue in place (fig. A).
3. Staple lid to cardboard base (fig. A).
4. Spray picture with hair spray and sprinkle with glitter.

Figure A

18

Holiday Gifts and Decorations, © 1986

Ceramic Hand Soap Dish

Materials

Fist-size piece of ceramic clay
    (water base)
Glaze
Kiln
8″ × 8″ burlap cloth
Small knife
Pencil

Figure A

TURNED-UP EDGE

Procedure

1. Place clay on top of burlap. Pound clay until it is approximately ¼″ thick.
2. Place your hand on clay, fingers together, and trace around it with a pencil.
3. Cut out hand shape with knife and peel clay carefully from burlap.
4. Turn up edges of hand so it can hold soap (fig. A).
5. Allow to dry thoroughly. Then bisque fire in kiln, glaze, and fire again.

Holiday Gifts and Decorations, © 1986

Brick Bookends

Materials

Two red bricks
Two 12″ × 18″ pieces of white
    art paper
Watercolors
Sponge
Shellac or lacquer and brush

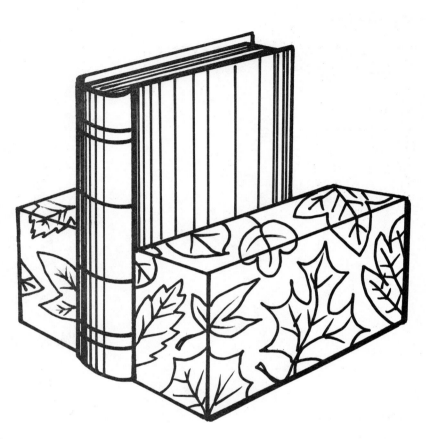

Procedure

1. Draw and color crayon leaf designs on art paper, filling both sheets.
2. Make a thin wash mixture by mixing paint with water.
3. Apply wash with wet sponge to cover both sheets of paper. Allow to dry.
4. Wrap the two bricks completely with the decorated art paper and glue in place.
5. Apply a coat of shellac or lacquer to each brick.

Holiday Gifts and Decorations, © 1986

Paintbrush Calendar

Materials

Pattern (p. 22)
Art paper:
    6″ × 10″ red (brush)
    4½″ × 5″ black (bristles)
1″ × 5″ aluminum foil (trim)
6″ × 10″ tagboard
Hole punch
Small desk calendar

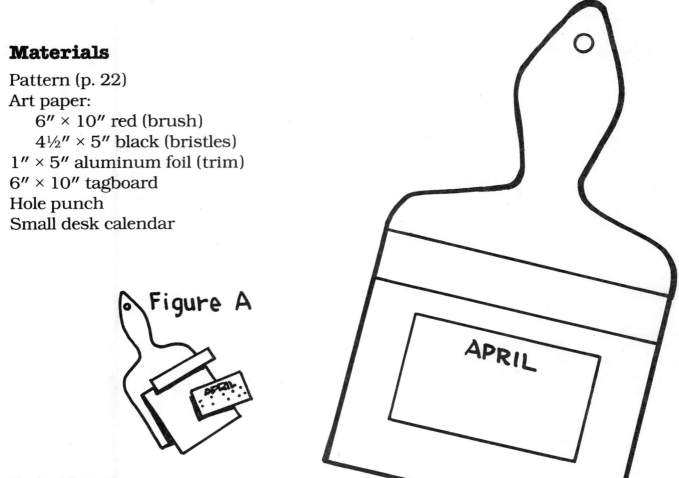

Figure A

Procedure

1. Trace brush pattern on red paper.
2. Glue red paper to tagboard and cut out along lines.
3. Glue on black paper for bristles. Trim off excess. Glue aluminum foil in place (fig. A).
4. Glue calendar in place.
5. Punch hole at top of handle for hanging.

Holiday Gifts and Decorations, © 1986

PAINTBRUSH
RED
(CUT 1)

GLUE CALENDAR
HERE

Owl Calendar

Materials

Patterns (p. 24)
Art paper:
    6″ × 9″ white (owl)
    4″ × 6″ brown (calendar)
9″ × 12″ tagboard
Two plastic eyes (optional)
Small desk calendar
Tagboard scrap

REAR VIEW

GLUE

Figure B

Figure A

JULY

		1	2	3	4	5
6	7	8	9	10	11	12
13	14	15	16	17	18	19
20	21	22	23	24	25	26
27	28	29	30	31		

Holiday Gifts and Decorations, © 1986

Procedure

1. Trace owl pattern on white paper with black felt pen.
2. Draw details and color with crayons or felt pens.
3. Glue owl to tagboard and cut out.
4. Glue plastic or art-paper eyes in place.
5. Trace calendar holder pattern on brown paper. Glue brown paper to tagboard and cut out.
6. Trace hanger pattern on tagboard scrap. Cut out.
7. Glue calendar holder and hanger to back of owl (fig. B).
8. Glue calendar to calendar holder (fig. A).

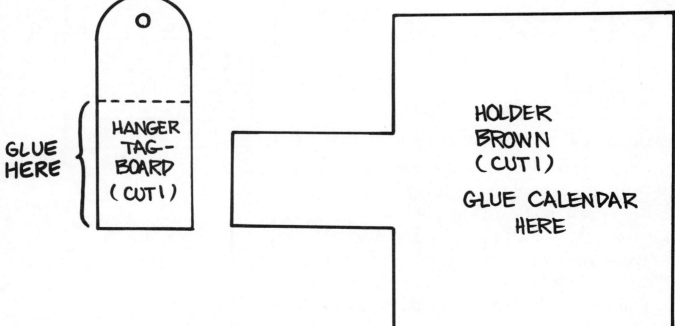

GLUE
HERE

HANGER
TAG-
BOARD
(CUT 1)

HOLDER
BROWN
(CUT 1)

GLUE CALENDAR
HERE

Kitty Calendar

Materials

Patterns (p. 26)
6″ × 9″ yellow art paper (kitty)
6″ × 9″ tagboard
Two plastic eyes (optional)
Small desk calendar
Tagboard scrap

Figure A

Procedure

1. Trace kitty pattern on yellow paper with black felt pen.
2. Color markings with brown felt pen or crayon.
3. Glue kitty to tagboard and cut out.
4. Glue plastic eyes in place, or draw them with crayon or felt pen.
5. Glue calendar in place (fig. A).
6. Trace hanger pattern on tagboard scrap, cut out, and glue to back of kitty.

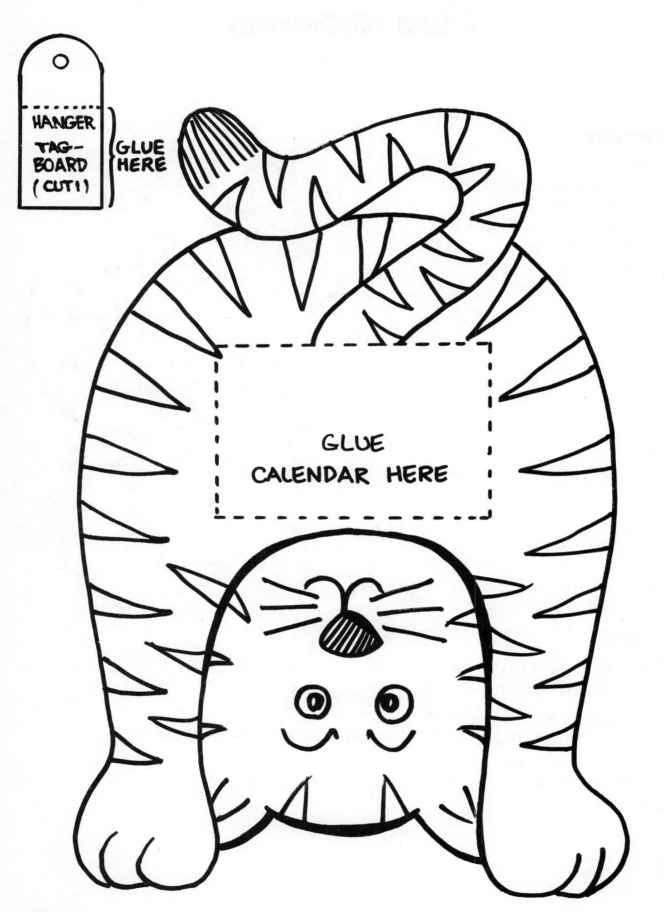

HANGER TAG-BOARD (CUT 1)

GLUE HERE

GLUE CALENDAR HERE

Cat Notepad

Materials

Patterns (p. 28)
8″ × 9″ wallpaper (cat and
    pencil holder)
4½″ × 3½″ red art paper (bow)
7″ × 9″ tagboard
One plastic eye (optional)
2½″ × 3″ cut-up typing paper
    (about 20 pieces)

Figure B

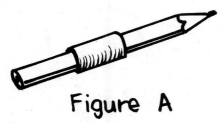

Figure A

Procedure

1. Trace cat pattern on wallpaper with black felt pen. Draw details.
2. Glue cat to tagboard and cut out.
3. Glue plastic or art-paper eye. Staple notepad (typing paper) in place.
4. Trace and cut out bow from red art paper.
5. Glue bow in place.
6. Use pencil holder pattern to cut out a small strip of wallpaper. Roll it around a pencil and glue to make pencil holder (fig. A).
7. Glue pencil holder to bow (fig. B).

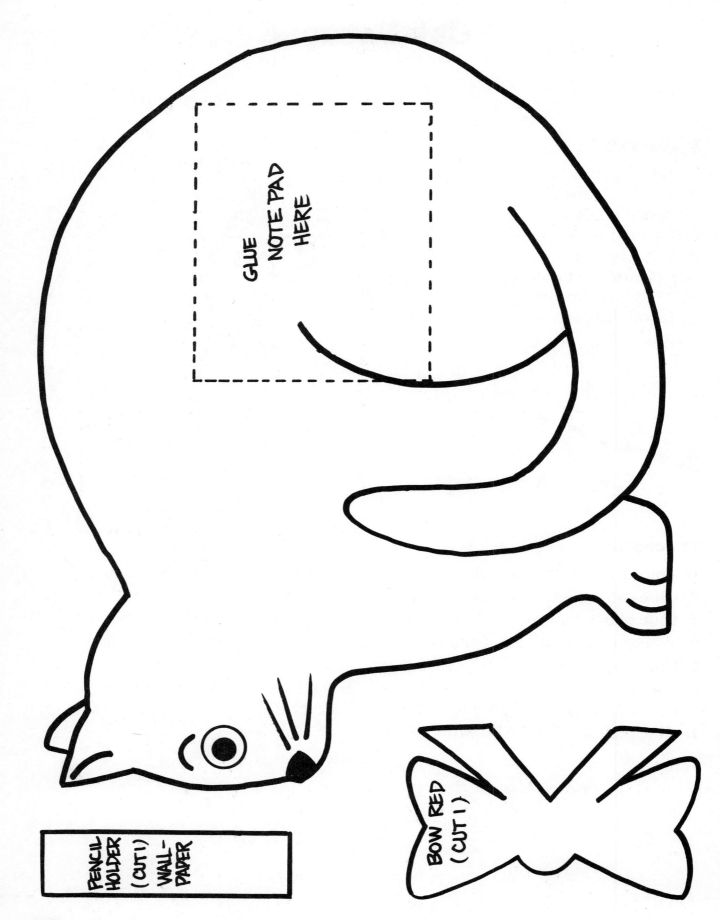

GLUE NOTE PAD HERE

PENCIL HOLDER
(CUT 1)
WALL-PAPER

BOW RED
(CUT 1)

28 *Cat Notepad*

Photo Calendar or Notepad

Materials

6½″ × 10½″ wallpaper
Art paper:
    4¼″ × 8¼″ of any color
      (backing)
    4″ × 4″ of any color (photo
      mount)
4½″ × 8½″ tagboard
12″ length of yarn or string
Small pencil
Hole punch
Photo or magazine picture
Small desk calendar or
    notepad
Hanger pattern (p. 30)

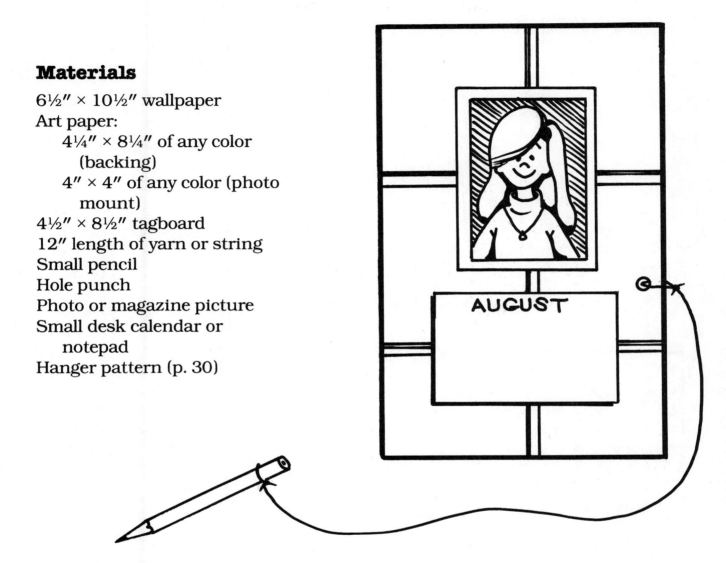

Procedure

1. Cover tagboard with wallpaper. Glue in place as shown on page 30 (figs. A and B).
2. Finish back by gluing 4¼″ × 8¼″ piece of art paper over folded flaps (figs. B and C).
3. Mount photo on 4″ × 4″ art paper and trim to ¼″ margin (fig. D).
4. Glue picture and calendar or notepad in place (fig. E).
5. Punch a hole to attach string or yarn and pencil (fig. E).
6. Tie pencil to end of string or yarn. Apply a drop of glue to help hold pencil in place.
7. If you wish to hang notepad, trace hanger pattern on tagboard scrap and cut out. Glue to back of notepad.

Holiday Gifts and Decorations, © 1986

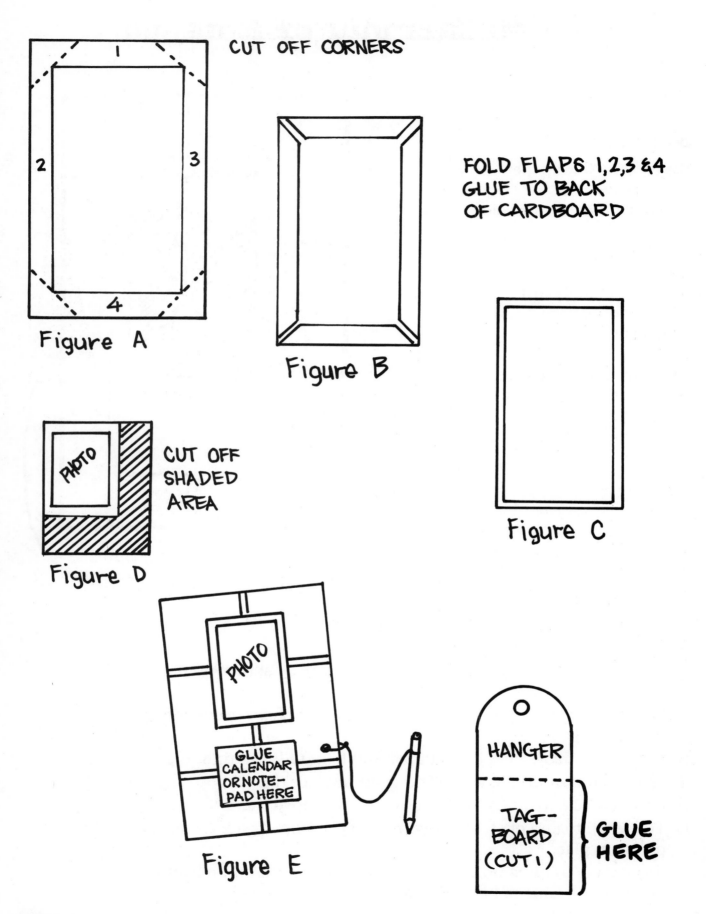

CUT OFF CORNERS

Figure A

FOLD FLAPS 1,2,3 &4
GLUE TO BACK
OF CARDBOARD

Figure B

Figure C

CUT OFF
SHADED
AREA

Figure D

PHOTO

GLUE
CALENDAR
OR NOTE-
PAD HERE

Figure E

HANGER

TAG-
BOARD
(CUT 1)

GLUE
HERE

Holiday Gifts and Decorations, © 1986

Mother's Day Cards

Materials

Patterns (p. 32)
9″ × 12″ art paper of various
   colors

Procedure

1. Fold one piece of 9″ × 12″ art paper in half to 9″ × 6″.
2. Trace patterns on art paper and cut out.
3. Glue shoe cutout in place on front cover of card (fig. A). Then glue flower and leaf cutouts in place as shown (fig. B).
4. Color and draw details with crayons or felt pens.
5. Print greetings inside card with black felt pen.

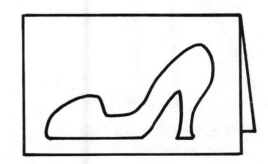

Figure A

Figure B

Holiday Gifts and Decorations, © 1986

LEAF GREEN
(CUT 4)

FLOWER ANY COLOR
(CUT 3)

SHOE ANY COLOR
(CUT 1)

Father's Day Cards

Materials

Patterns (pp. 34–35)
9″ × 12″ art paper of various
colors
9″ × 12″ black art paper

Procedure

1. Fold one piece of 9″ × 12″ art paper in half to 9″ × 6″.
2. Select a silhouette pattern, trace it on black art paper, and cut out.
3. Glue cutout to front cover of card.
4. Print greetings inside card with felt pen.

34 *Father's Day Cards*

Holiday Gifts and Decorations, © 1986

Christmas Shape Greeting Cards

Materials

Patterns (pp. 37–38)
Art paper:
   10″ × 12″ of any color
    (ornament)
   9″ × 12″ white (candy cane)
   6″ × 16″ green (holly)
   red scraps

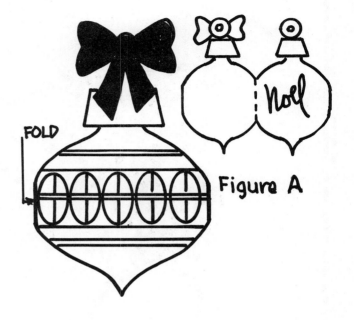

Figure A

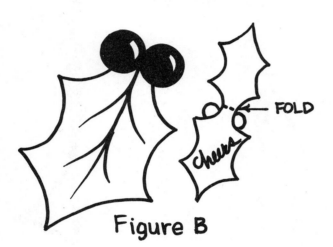

Figure B

Figure C

Procedure

1. Choose pattern and fold art paper accordingly.
2. Place pattern on paper fold where indicated (figs. A–C). Trace pattern and cut out.
3. Cut details (berries, bow) from scraps of art paper and glue in place.
4. Draw details with crayons or felt pens.
5. Write greetings inside card with black felt pen.

Holiday Gifts and Decorations, © 1986

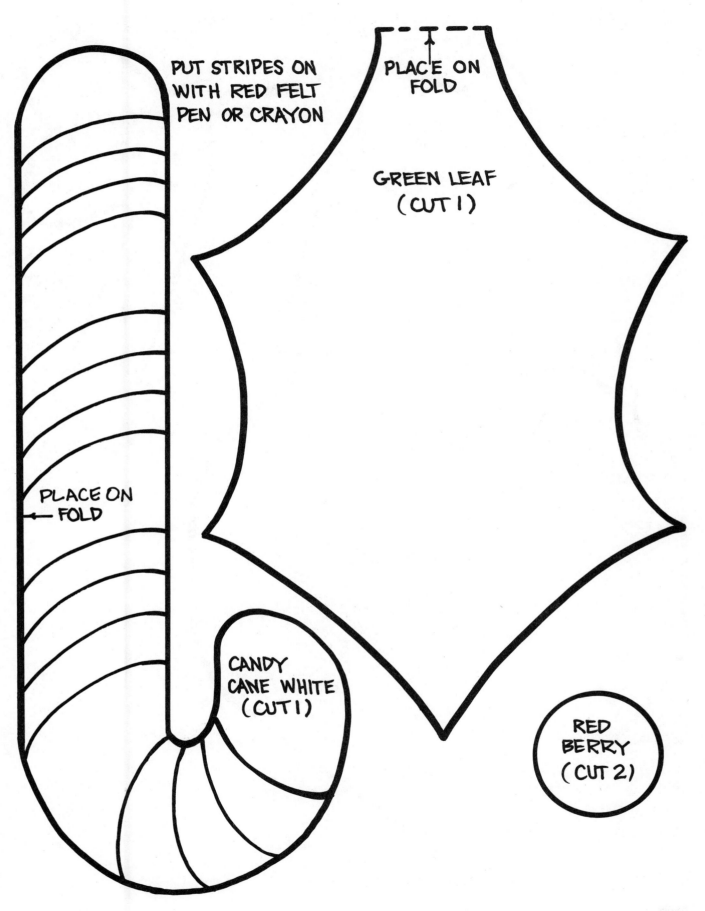

PUT STRIPES ON WITH RED FELT PEN OR CRAYON

PLACE ON FOLD

GREEN LEAF (CUT 1)

PLACE ON FOLD

CANDY CANE WHITE (CUT 1)

RED BERRY (CUT 2)

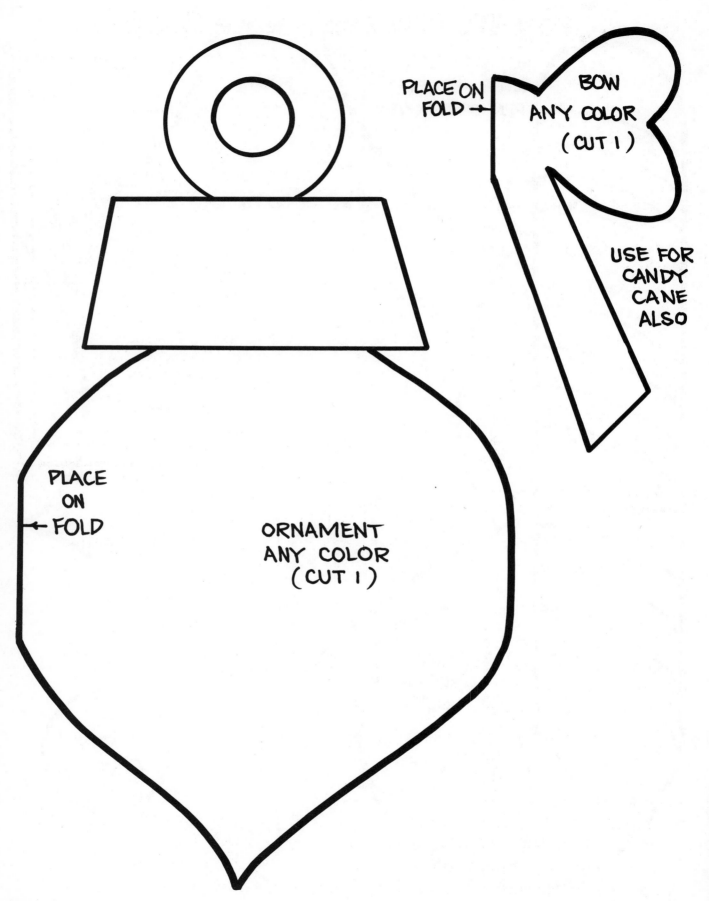

PLACE ON
FOLD →

BOW
ANY COLOR
(CUT 1)

USE FOR
CANDY
CANE
ALSO

PLACE
ON
← FOLD

ORNAMENT
ANY COLOR
(CUT 1)

Pop-Up Winter Scene Card

Materials

Patterns (p. 40)
Art paper:
  9″ × 12″ blue (card)
  8″ × 11″ white (scene)
  6″ × 9″ white (figures)
Hair spray
Gold or silver glitter

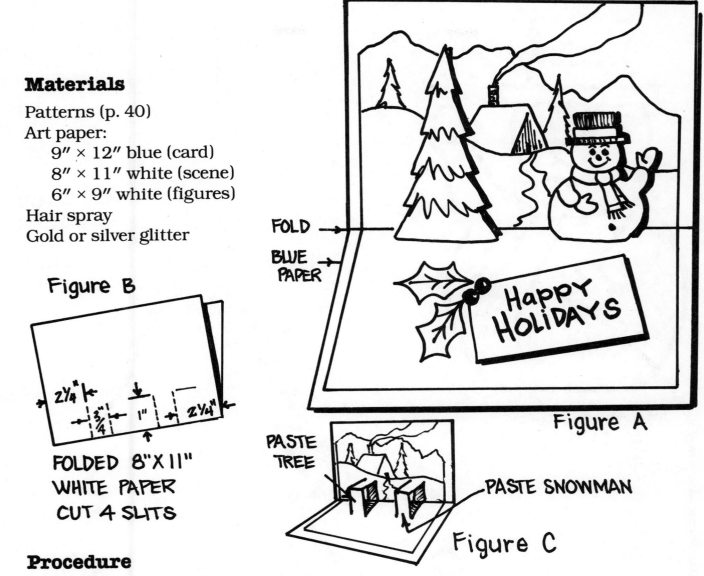

Figure B

FOLDED 8″X11″
WHITE PAPER
CUT 4 SLITS

FOLD
BLUE PAPER

Figure A

PASTE TREE
PASTE SNOWMAN

Figure C

Procedure

1. Fold blue paper and 8″ × 11″ white paper in half to 8″ × 5½″.
2. Draw winter scene on upper half of white paper with pencil. Outline with black felt pen.
3. Cut away along upper edge of the drawing (fig. A).
4. On fold of 8″ × 11″ white paper, cut four slits according to the dimensions shown (fig. B).
5. Fold slit pieces out (fig. C).
6. Trace snowman, tree, holly, and berries on white paper. Color with crayons or felt pens, and cut out. Glue to slit pieces as shown (figs. A and C). Write *Happy Holidays* on white paper and cut out.
7. Glue scene to blue paper (fig. A).
8. Spray inside of card with hair spray and sprinkle with glitter.

SNOWMAN
(CUT 1)

BERRIES
(CUT 2)

HOLLY
(CUT 2)

TREE
(CUT 1)

Pasta Angel Ornament

Materials

Two pieces elbow macaroni
   (arms)
One piece rigatoni (body)
One piece bowtie pasta (wings)
Salad macaroni (hair)
Wooden bead (20 mm)
3″ gold pipe cleaner
6″ gold wire cord
Plasticine clay
White enamel spray paint

Figure E → WIRE
← PIPE CLEANER

Figure A

Figure B

Figure C

FRONT
BACK
Figure D

Procedure

1. Fill hole in bead with clay. Glue bead to rigatoni (fig. A). Allow to dry.
2. Glue on bowtie wings (fig. B). Allow to dry.
3. Glue on elbow macaroni arms (fig. C). Allow to dry.
4. Glue on salad macaroni for hair. Be sure to leave a small space over bead hole uncovered (fig. D). Allow to dry.
5. Spray with white enamel paint and allow to dry.
6. Twist 3″ piece of pipe cleaner around index finger for halo. Glue on head (fig. E).
7. Bend gold wire cord in half and insert into clay filling for hanger (fig. E).
8. Draw on face with felt pen.

Holiday Gifts and Decorations, © 1986

Mosaic Greeting Card

Materials

Art paper:
  9″ × 12″ white
  5″ × 8″ black (trim)
Used greeting card
Ruler

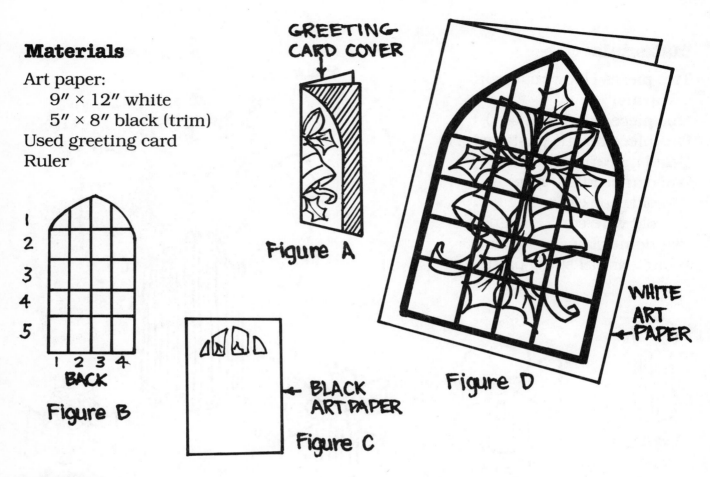

GREETING CARD COVER

Figure A

Figure B

BLACK ART PAPER

Figure C

WHITE ART PAPER

Figure D

Procedure

1. Fold white paper in half to 9″ × 6″.
2. Cut used greeting card in half along the fold. Fold cover of greeting card in half lengthwise and cut it in the shape of a cathedral stained glass window (fig. A). Unfold.
3. Draw lines on back of greeting card cover, dividing it into sections (fig. B).
4. Cut out top four pieces and glue to black paper, colored side up. Leave ⅛″ space between each piece. Trim pieces to fit if necessary (fig. C).
5. Continue this procedure until all pieces have been cut and glued in place. (Do not cut all pieces at once as this is too confusing.) Allow to dry.
6. Trim black paper around edge of window shape, allowing ⅛″ border.
7. Glue to white paper for a new mosaic-design greeting card (fig. D).
8. Cut and glue greeting of old card inside new card.

Holiday Gifts and Decorations, © 1986

Melted Crayon Thank-You Notes

Materials

Old electric fry pan
Art paper:
    six 4″ × 10″ white
      (note cards)
    six 3½″ × 4¼″ black
      (mounting paper)
Six pieces 4¼″ × 5¼″ typing
    paper (crayon design)
Paper towels or clean cloth
Used crayons
Six 4¼″ × 5″ envelopes

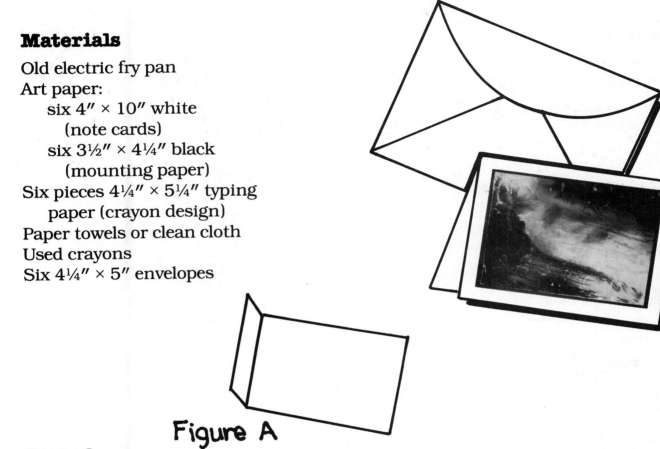

Figure A

Procedure

1. Set pan temperature at 250 degrees.
2. With a crayon, draw a small circle in center of pan. Then draw another circle around the first one, using a different color. Continue this until five circles, each one a different color, are drawn.
3. Make a one-inch-deep fold along short edge of typing paper. Use this as a handle when you apply paper to melted crayon (fig. A).
4. Lay paper on top of melted crayon, then lift it off.
5. Wipe crayon residue from pan with cloth or paper towel.
6. Apply a different combination of crayon colors to pan and make another printing on second piece of typing paper. Make six printings in all for six notes.
7. Fold 4″ × 10″ white paper in half to 4″ × 5″.
8. Glue black paper to front of folded white paper.
9. Trim melted crayon designs to 3″ × 4″ and glue them to black paper. Lay several books on top and allow to dry.

Paper Plate Bird Pictures

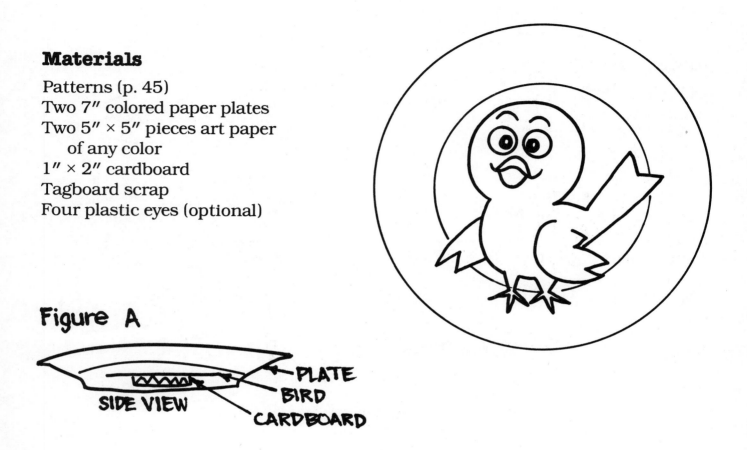

Materials

Patterns (p. 45)
Two 7″ colored paper plates
Two 5″ × 5″ pieces art paper
   of any color
1″ × 2″ cardboard
Tagboard scrap
Four plastic eyes (optional)

Figure A

SIDE VIEW

PLATE
BIRD
CARDBOARD

Procedure

1. Trace bird patterns on art paper with felt pen. Cut out.
2. Glue 1″ × 1″ piece of cardboard to back of each cutout bird. Then glue each bird to center of a paper plate (fig. A). This creates a 3-D effect.
3. Glue plastic or art-paper eyes in place.
4. Trace hanger pattern on tagboard scrap, cut out two, and glue to backs of paper plates (fig. B).

Figure B
BACK VIEW

Holiday Gifts and Decorations, © 1986

BIRD ANY COLOR
(CUT 1)

BIRD ANY COLOR
(CUT 1)

GLUE
AREA

TAGBOARD
HANGER
(CUT 2)

Friendly Fruits and Veggies Plaques

Materials

Patterns (p. 47)
6″ × 9″ white art paper
Tagboard scrap
6″ × 9″ tagboard
3″ × 4″ cardboard
7″-diameter paper plate for
    each plaque
Two plastic eyes (optional)

Procedure

1. Trace fruit or vegetable pattern on white paper with black felt pen.
2. Glue white paper to tagboard and cut out along lines.
3. Color drawing with crayons or felt pens.
4. Glue plastic eyes in place, or draw them with crayon or felt pen. Draw mouth, nose, and eyebrows with black felt pen.
5. Trace arm and leg patterns on scraps of art paper, cut out, and glue in place.
6. Cut two 1″ × 2″ pieces of cardboard, glue them together, and then glue to back of cutout. This gives a 3–D effect.
7. Glue fruit or vegetable to center of paper plate.
8. Trace hanger pattern on tagboard scrap and cut out. Glue to back of paper plate.

Holiday Gifts and Decorations, © 1986

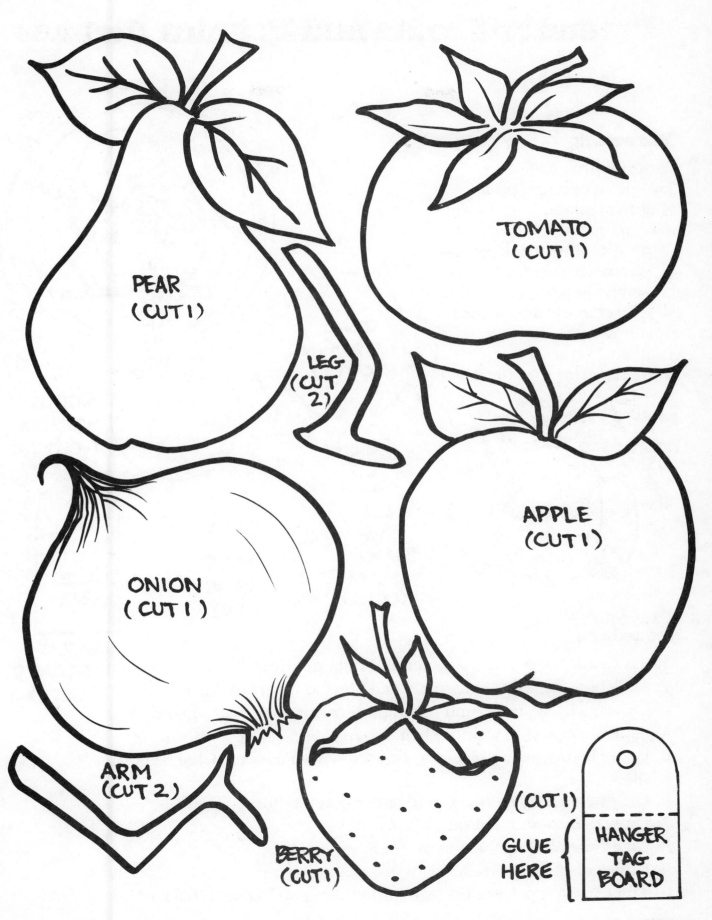

PEAR
(CUT 1)

TOMATO
(CUT 1)

LEG
(CUT 2)

APPLE
(CUT 1)

ONION
(CUT 1)

ARM
(CUT 2)

BERRY
(CUT 1)

(CUT 1)

GLUE HERE

HANGER TAG-BOARD

Jar Lid and Walnut Shell Owl

Materials

Patterns (this page)
Two-piece canning jar lid
½ walnut shell
Art paper:
    4″ × 4″ blue (background)
    3″ × 3″ brown (owl)
    scraps of black and yellow
      (feet, beak, and moon)
Small twig
Tagboard scrap
Two plastic eyes (optional)

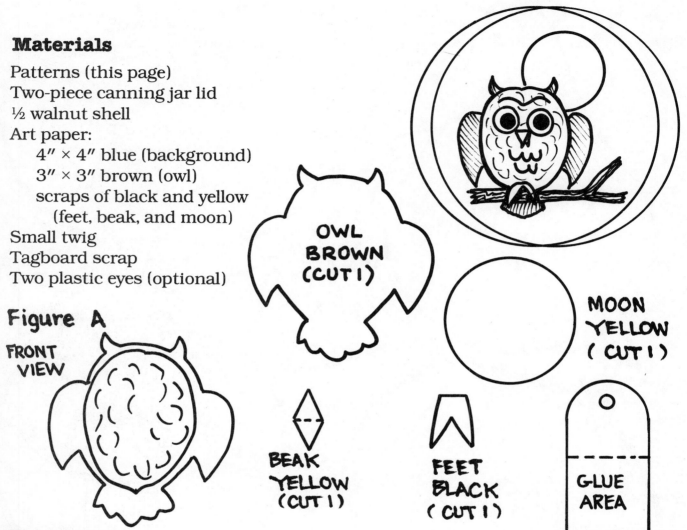

Figure A

FRONT VIEW

OWL BROWN (CUT 1)

MOON YELLOW (CUT 1)

BEAK YELLOW (CUT 1)

FEET BLACK (CUT 1)

GLUE AREA

HANGER TAGBOARD (CUT 1)

Procedure

1. Trace lid insert on blue paper and cut out circle.
2. Glue blue circle to lid insert. Then glue lid insert inside ring.
3. Trace owl, feet, beak, and moon patterns on art paper and cut out.
4. Glue paper owl to walnut shell (fig. A).
5. Glue plastic eyes in place, or draw eyes with felt pen. Glue beak in place.
6. Glue moon and walnut owl to paper-covered lid.
7. Draw details with felt pen.
8. Glue twig in place.
9. Glue feet in place.
10. Trace hanger pattern on tagboard and cut out. Glue to back of lid.

Holiday Gifts and Decorations, © 1986

Jar Lid Butterflies

Materials

Pattern (this page)
Two-piece canning jar lids (2)
Art paper:
    four 4″ × 4″ of any color
        (background and
        butterflies)
    1¼″ × 10″ yellow (ribbon)
Tagboard scrap

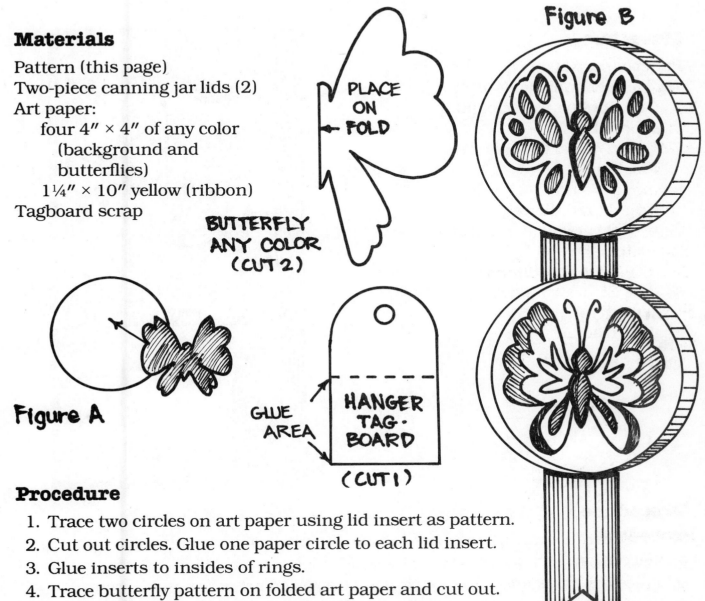

PLACE ON FOLD

BUTTERFLY ANY COLOR (CUT 2)

Figure A

GLUE AREA

HANGER TAG- BOARD

(CUT 1)

Figure B

Procedure

1. Trace two circles on art paper using lid insert as pattern.
2. Cut out circles. Glue one paper circle to each lid insert.
3. Glue inserts to insides of rings.
4. Trace butterfly pattern on folded art paper and cut out.
5. Use black felt pen to draw designs on butterflies' wings.
6. Color wings with crayons or felt pens.
7. Glue butterflies on paper circles (fig. A). Draw antennae with black felt pen.
8. Cut an inverted "V" at one end of 1¼″ × 10″ art paper. Add details with black crayon or felt pens.
9. Glue lids to paper ribbon (fig. B).
10. Trace hanger pattern on tagboard scrap and cut out. Glue to back of top lid.

Floral Design

Materials

Patterns (p. 51)

7½″ × 10½″ wallpaper or
Con-Tact paper (woodgrain,
if possible)

7½″ × 10½″ cardboard
(backing)

Art paper:
  4″ × 4″ red (flowerpot)
  6″ × 9″ green (leaves and
    stems)
  5″ × 5″ yellow (flowers)
  3″ × 3″ brown (flower
    centers)

Tagboard scrap

Procedure

1. Cover cardboard with wallpaper or Con-Tact paper. Glue or press in place. (Con-Tact paper is self-adhesive.)
2. Trace flowers, stems, leaves, and pot patterns on art paper and cut out.
3. Arrange cutouts on covered cardboard and glue in place.
4. Trace hanger pattern on tagboard scrap, cut out, and glue to back of picture.

Holiday Gifts and Decorations, © 1986

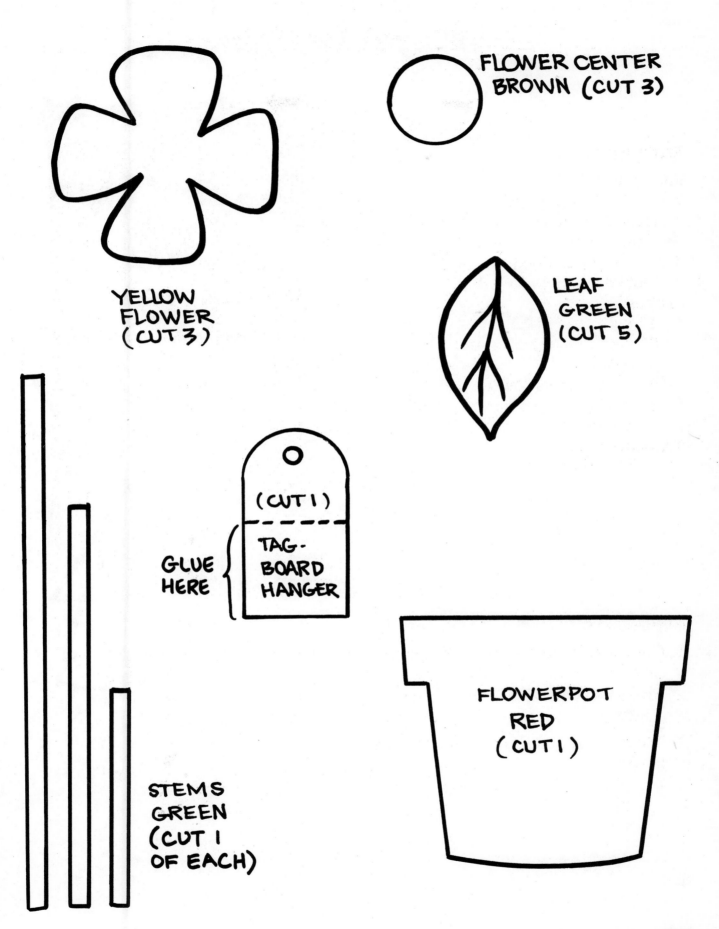

YELLOW FLOWER (CUT 3)

FLOWER CENTER BROWN (CUT 3)

LEAF GREEN (CUT 5)

(CUT 1)

GLUE HERE

TAG-BOARD HANGER

STEMS GREEN (CUT 1 OF EACH)

FLOWERPOT RED (CUT 1)

Wallpaper Fish

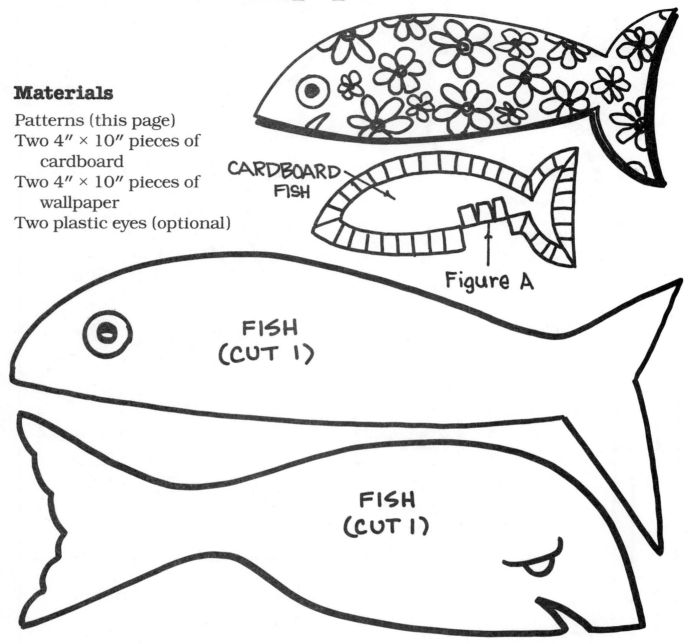

Materials

Patterns (this page)
Two 4″ × 10″ pieces of
  cardboard
Two 4″ × 10″ pieces of
  wallpaper
Two plastic eyes (optional)

CARDBOARD FISH

Figure A

FISH
(CUT 1)

FISH
(CUT 1)

Procedure

1. Trace fish patterns on cardboard and cut out.
2. Glue cutouts on back side of wallpaper and trace around them, allowing an extra 1½″ around each fish shape (fig. A). Cut around outline.
3. Cut slits around edge of fish as shown (fig. A).
4. Fold slit pieces back over to cardboard and glue in place (fig. A).
5. Glue plastic or art-paper eyes in place.
6. For display, stick straight pins through fish so that only about ⅛″ of pin penetrates wall. This creates a 3-D effect.

Holiday Gifts and Decorations, © 1986.

Framed Miniwatercolor

Materials

Art paper:
    4½″ × 6″ white
      (background)
    4½″ × 12″ black (frame)
4½″ × 6″ tagboard
Watercolor set with two
    brushes—No. 7 and No. 12
Ruler

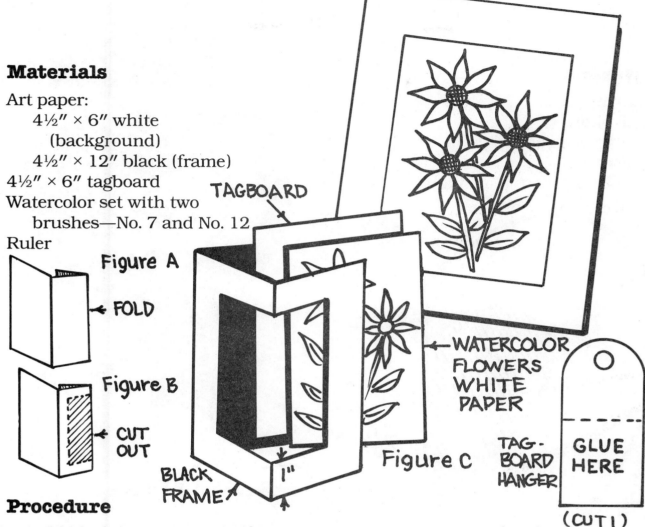

Figure A — FOLD

Figure B — CUT OUT

TAGBOARD

BLACK FRAME

1″

Figure C

WATERCOLOR FLOWERS WHITE PAPER

TAG-BOARD HANGER

GLUE HERE

(CUT 1)

Procedure

1. Fold black art paper in half to 4½″ × 6″. Open paper and fold front section in half again as shown (fig. A).

2. Cut out center of black paper, leaving 1″ margins on all sides (figs. B and C).

3. Place frame on white paper and trace around cutout edge for drawing area.

4. Remove frame from white paper.

5. Paint three spots on white paper for flower centers.

6. Paint petals of flowers by using side of No. 7 brush. (Avoid excessive use of water.)

7. Paint thin stems with fine tip of No. 7 brush. Paint leaves with side of No. 12 brush.

8. Glue painting between black frame and tagboard as shown (fig. C).

9. Trace hanger on tagboard scrap. Cut out and glue to back of painting.

Photos from the Heart

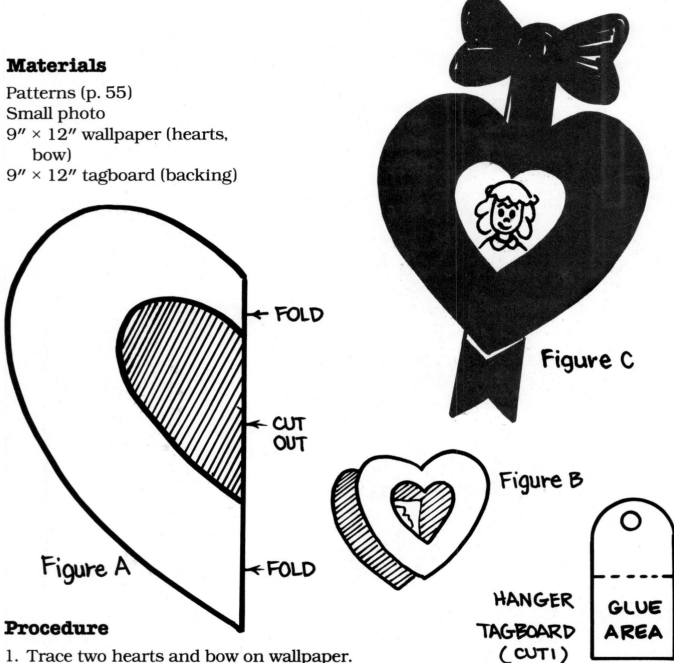

Materials

Patterns (p. 55)
Small photo
9″ × 12″ wallpaper (hearts, bow)
9″ × 12″ tagboard (backing)

← FOLD

← CUT OUT

Figure A

← FOLD

Figure C

Figure B

HANGER TAGBOARD (CUT 1)

GLUE AREA

Procedure

1. Trace two hearts and bow on wallpaper.
2. Glue wallpaper to tagboard and cut out along lines.
3. From the center of one heart, cut out a small heart to accommodate your photo (fig. A).
4. Glue photo in center of uncut heart (fig. B).
5. Glue the two hearts together as shown (fig. B).
6. Glue bow to back of hearts (fig. C).
7. Trace hanger on tagboard scrap, cut out, and glue to back of bow.

54

Holiday Gifts and Decorations, © 1986

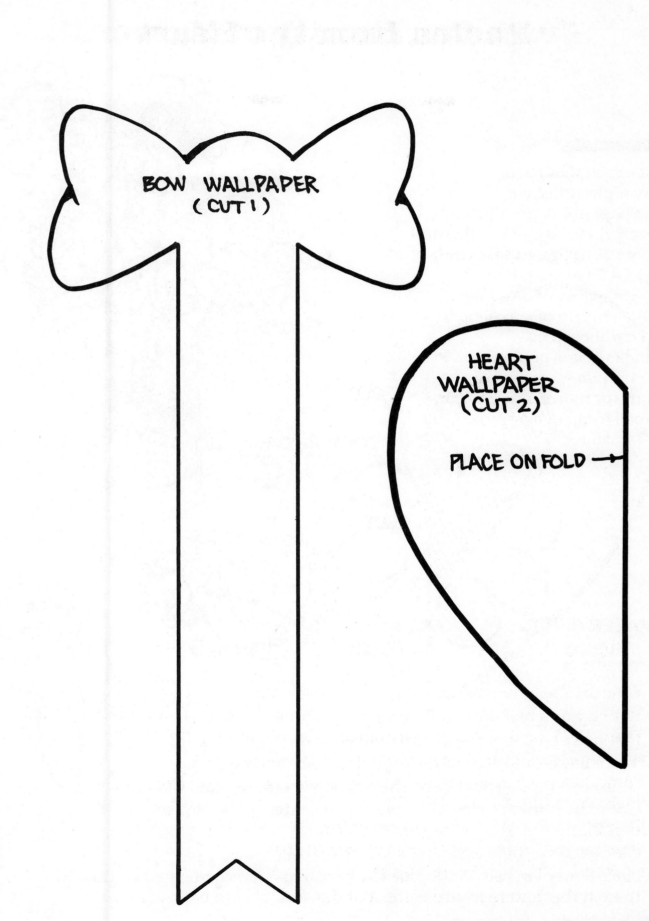

BOW WALLPAPER
(CUT 1)

HEART
WALLPAPER
(CUT 2)

PLACE ON FOLD →

Juice Can Family of Flowers

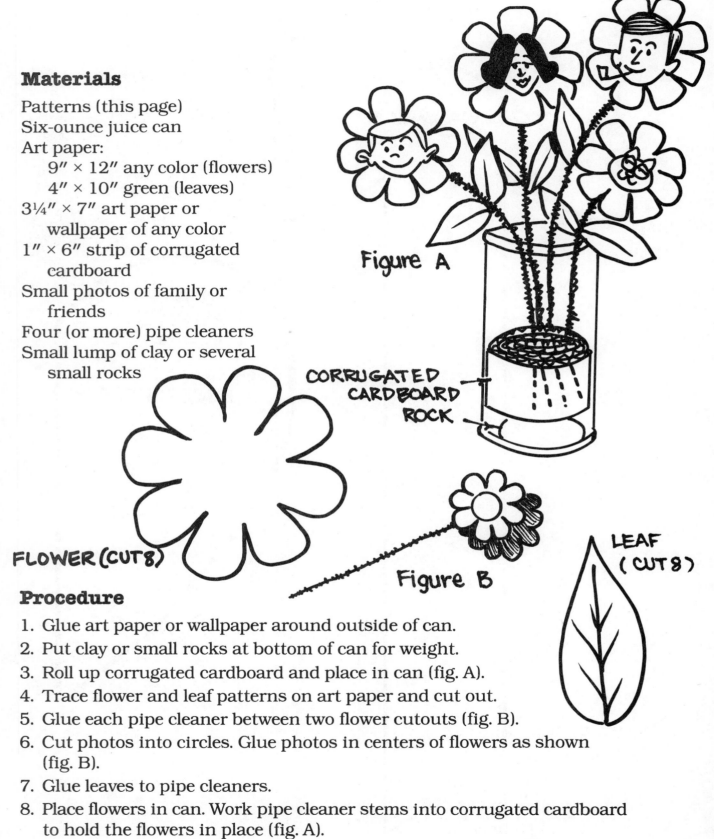

Materials

Patterns (this page)

Six-ounce juice can

Art paper:

    9″ × 12″ any color (flowers)

    4″ × 10″ green (leaves)

3¼″ × 7″ art paper or
    wallpaper of any color

1″ × 6″ strip of corrugated
    cardboard

Small photos of family or
    friends

Four (or more) pipe cleaners

Small lump of clay or several
    small rocks

Figure A

CORRUGATED
CARDBOARD
ROCK

FLOWER (CUT 8)

Figure B

LEAF
(CUT 8)

Procedure

1. Glue art paper or wallpaper around outside of can.
2. Put clay or small rocks at bottom of can for weight.
3. Roll up corrugated cardboard and place in can (fig. A).
4. Trace flower and leaf patterns on art paper and cut out.
5. Glue each pipe cleaner between two flower cutouts (fig. B).
6. Cut photos into circles. Glue photos in centers of flowers as shown (fig. B).
7. Glue leaves to pipe cleaners.
8. Place flowers in can. Work pipe cleaner stems into corrugated cardboard to hold the flowers in place (fig. A).

Holiday Gifts and Decorations, © 1986

Wallpaper Photo Display

Materials

5″ × 11″ wallpaper
2″ × 3″ art paper of any
    color (photo backing)
3″ × 9″ tagboard
Small photo or photocopy of
    photo
Stapler

Figure E

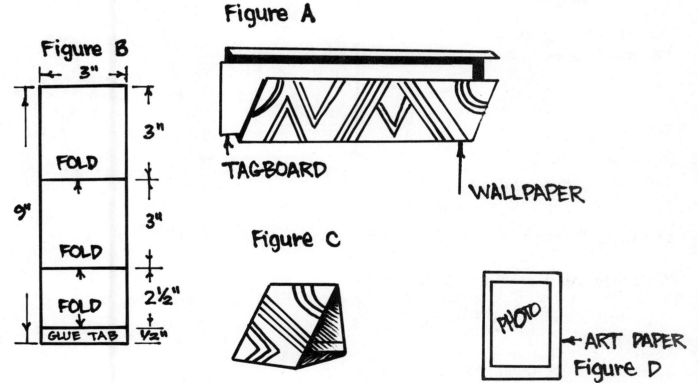

Figure A

TAGBOARD

WALLPAPER

Figure B

3″

3″

FOLD

3″

9″

FOLD

2½″

FOLD

GLUE TAB ½″

Figure C

Figure D

PHOTO

← ART PAPER

Procedure

1. Cover tagboard with wallpaper. Glue together as shown (fig. A).
2. Fold as shown (fig. B), and glue or staple together (fig. C).
3. Glue photo to art paper. Trim art paper to allow a ¼″ border (fig. D).
4. Glue photo in place on stand (fig. E).

Holiday Gifts and Decorations, © 1986

57

Schoolhouse or Apple Photo Display

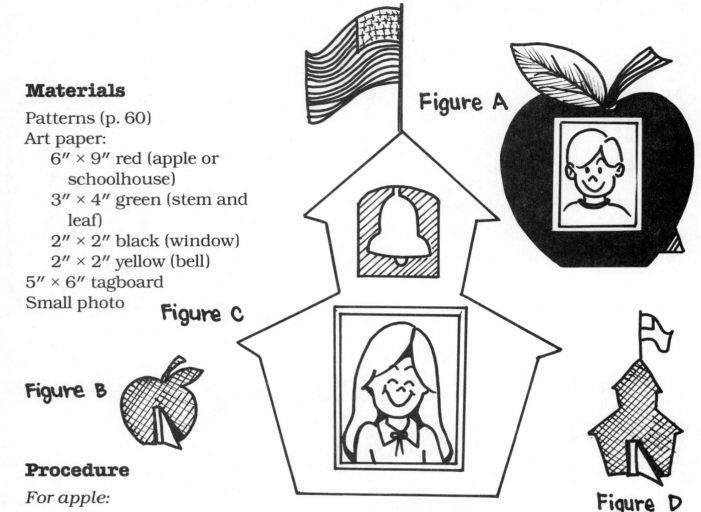

Figure A

Figure C

Figure B

Figure D

Materials

Patterns (p. 60)
Art paper:
    6″ × 9″ red (apple or
      schoolhouse)
    3″ × 4″ green (stem and
      leaf)
    2″ × 2″ black (window)
    2″ × 2″ yellow (bell)
5″ × 6″ tagboard
Small photo

Procedure

For apple:

1. Trace apple pattern including stem and leaf on red paper.
2. Glue red paper to tagboard and cut out apple.
3. Trace leaf and stem pattern on green paper. Cut out and glue in place on apple (fig. A).
4. Glue photo in center of apple (fig. A).
5. Trace stand on tagboard scrap and cut out. Fold where indicated and glue to back of apple (fig. B).

For schoolhouse:

1. Trace schoolhouse pattern on red paper.
2. Glue red paper to tagboard and cut out schoolhouse.
3. Trace bell pattern on yellow paper, and trace window pattern on black paper. Cut out and glue in place (fig. C).
4. Glue photo in center of schoolhouse.
5. Trace stand on tagboard scrap and cut out. Fold where indicated and glue to back of schoolhouse (fig. D).

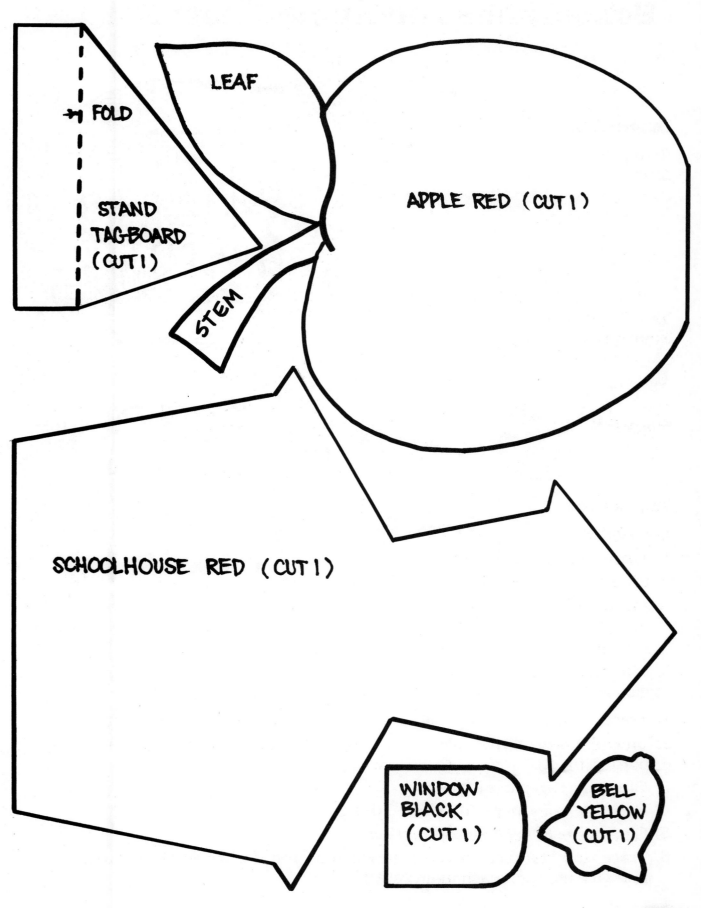

FOLD

LEAF

STAND
TAG-BOARD
(CUT 1)

STEM

APPLE RED (CUT 1)

SCHOOLHOUSE RED (CUT 1)

WINDOW
BLACK
(CUT 1)

BELL
YELLOW
(CUT 1)

Holiday Gifts and Decorations, © 1986

Jar Lid Photo Frame

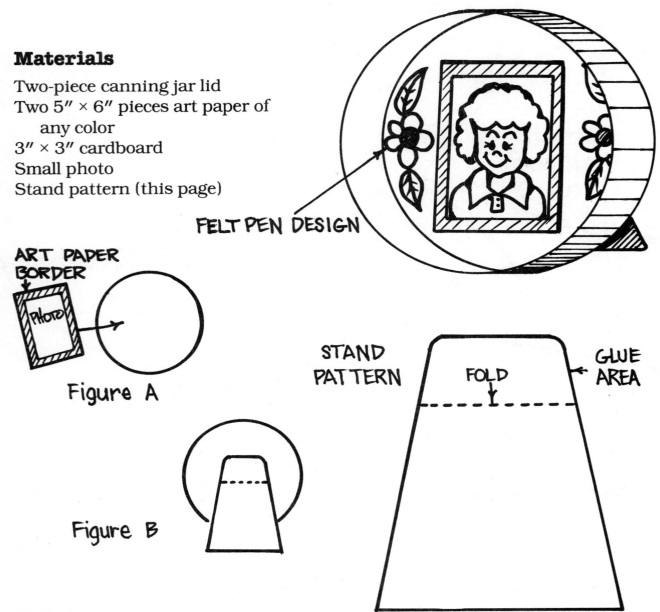

Materials

Two-piece canning jar lid
Two 5″ × 6″ pieces art paper of
   any color
3″ × 3″ cardboard
Small photo
Stand pattern (this page)

FELT PEN DESIGN

ART PAPER BORDER

PHOTO

Figure A

Figure B

STAND PATTERN

FOLD

GLUE AREA

Procedure

1. Trace lid insert on art paper and cut out. Glue paper circle to lid insert.
2. Glue photo to another piece of art paper. Trim art paper to allow a ¼″ border (fig. A).
3. Glue photo in place (fig. A).
4. Decorate art paper with felt pen design as shown.
5. Glue lid insert to inside of lid ring.
6. Trace stand pattern on cardboard and cut out. Fold where indicated and glue stand to back of lid insert (fig. B).

60

Holiday Gifts and Decorations, © 1986

Christmas Card Ball

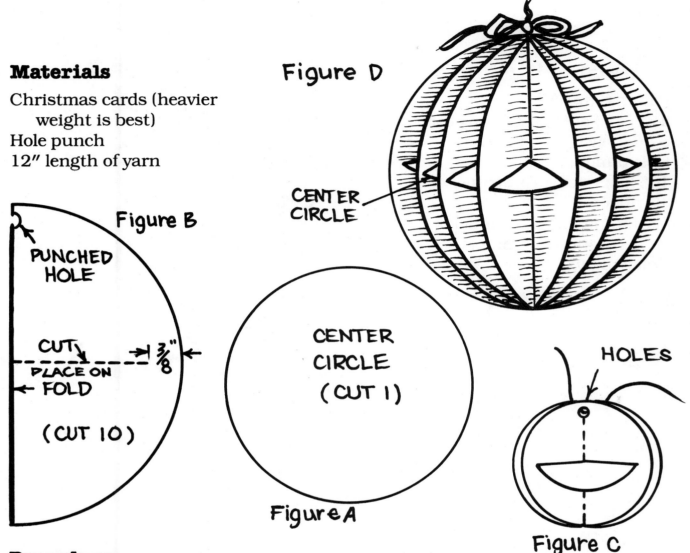

Figure D

CENTER
CIRCLE

Figure B

PUNCHED
HOLE

CUT
PLACE ON
FOLD
$\frac{3}{8}$"

(CUT 10)

CENTER
CIRCLE
(CUT 1)

Figure A

HOLES

Figure C

Materials

Christmas cards (heavier
   weight is best)
Hole punch
12″ length of yarn

Procedure

1. Use figures A and B as patterns. Trace one smaller circle (fig. A) and ten larger circles (fig. B) on Christmas cards. Cut out.
2. Fold the ten larger circles in half and cut a line from their centers to ⅜″ from the edges (fig. B).
3. Open two of the larger circles and punch a hole at the outer edge of each one on the fold line (fig. C).
4. Slip the smaller circle through the cut on each of the two larger circles (fig. C), with the folds facing center and aligning the punched-out holes. Thread a 12″ piece of yarn through both holes and tie for hanging.
5. Slip the cut on each of the eight remaining folded circles one by one on the center circle. Open each circle up slightly to complete the ornament (fig. D).

Holiday Gifts and Decorations, © 1986

Personalized Ornaments

Materials

Patterns (p. 63)
4½" × 9" art paper of any color
    (for each ornament)
Hole punch
10" length of yarn, string, or
    ribbon
Glitter, rickrack, sequins for
    decoration (optional)
Small photo

Procedure

For each ornament:

1. Fold art paper in half to 4½" × 4½" and glue together for more strength.
2. Trace pattern on art paper and cut out.
3. Glue photo in place.
4. Punch hole in top of ornament and thread yarn through. Tie ends together.
5. Decorate with available materials.

Holiday Gifts and Decorations, © 1986

Personalized Ornaments **63**

Wire Hanger Christmas Card Holder

Materials

Patterns (p. 66)
Wire hanger
Art paper:
> 12″ × 18″ red (to cover
>   hanger)
> 7″ × 10″ red (hat)
> 12″ × 18″ white (holder)
> 9″ × 12″ white (mustache,
>   beard, hatband, pom-pom,
>   cuffs)
> 5″ × 5″ pink (face, nose)
> 3″ × 6″ green (mittens)

Two plastic eyes (optional)
Red chalk

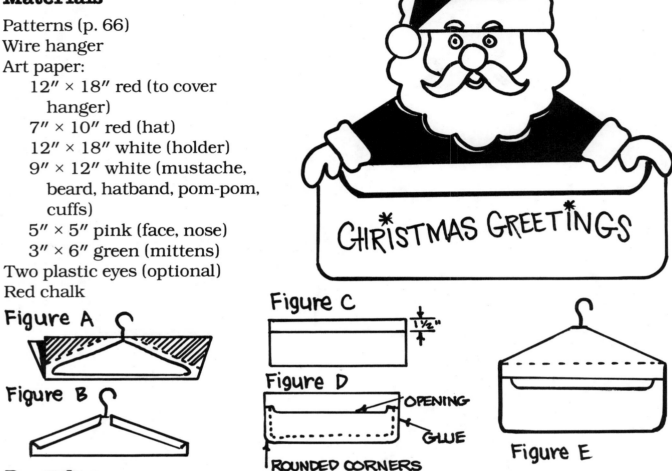

Figure A

Figure B

Figure C

Figure D — OPENING / GLUE / ROUNDED CORNERS

Figure E

Procedure

1. Fold 12″ × 18″ red paper in half to 6″ × 18″. Insert hanger and trim off corners of red paper, leaving ¾″-wide flaps (fig. A). Fold flaps over hanger and glue together on back (fig. B).
2. To make card holder, fold one long edge of 12″ × 18″ white paper to within 1½″ of other long edge as shown (fig. C). Cut out holder opening and round off bottom corners (fig. D). Glue outer edges of holder (fig. D).
3. Glue holder to bottom edge of paper-covered hanger (fig. E).
4. Trace patterns on art paper and cut out.
5. Glue beard, mustache, and nose on face. Draw eyebrows with black felt pen. Rub red chalk on cheeks.
6. Glue on plastic or art-paper eyes.
7. Glue on hatband, folded hat, and pom-pom. Glue head to top of hanger.
8. Glue on mittens and cuffs.
9. Print *Christmas Greetings* with red and green felt pens on holder.

64

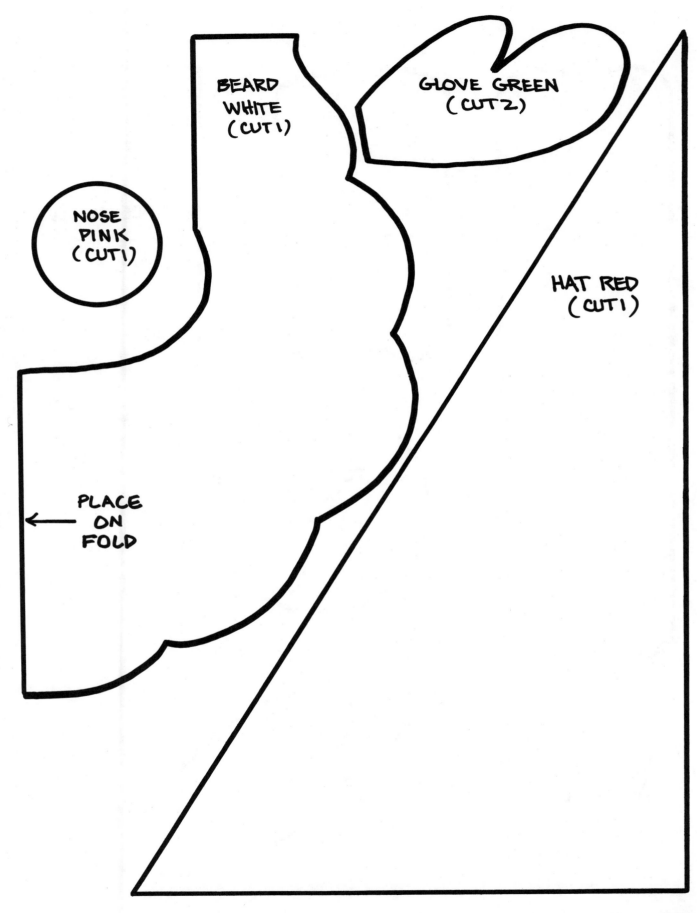

BEARD
WHITE
(CUT 1)

GLOVE GREEN
(CUT 2)

NOSE
PINK
(CUT 1)

HAT RED
(CUT 1)

← PLACE
ON
FOLD

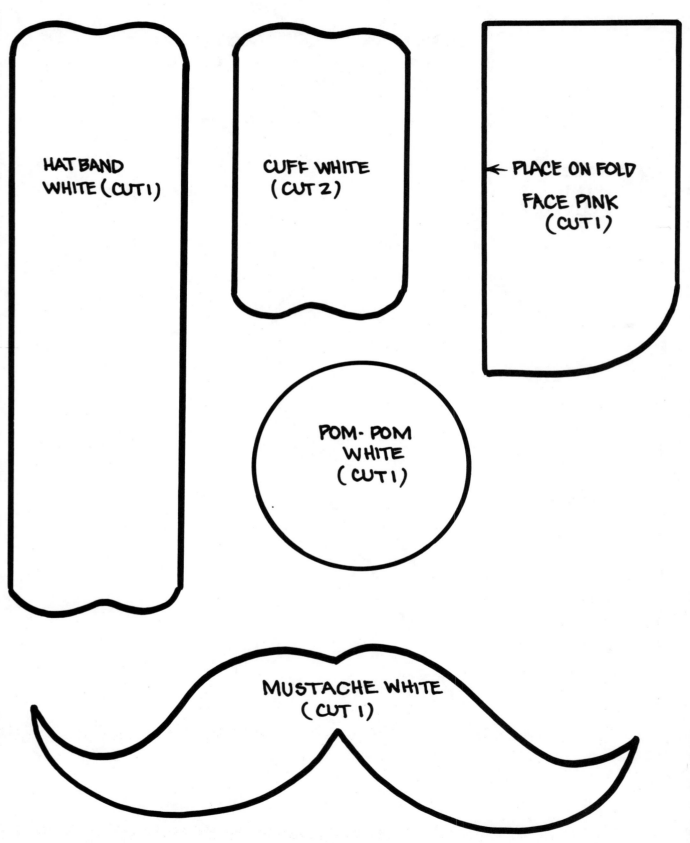

HAT BAND
WHITE (CUT 1)

CUFF WHITE
(CUT 2)

← PLACE ON FOLD
FACE PINK
(CUT 1)

POM-POM
WHITE
(CUT 1)

MUSTACHE WHITE
(CUT 1)

Holiday Gifts and Decorations, © 1986

Snowman or Santa Soap Box Card Holder

Materials

Patterns (pp. 69–70)

Giant-size (49-ounce) laundry detergent box

Art paper:

For snowman:

two 12″ × 18″ white (box and snowman)

6″ × 9″ red (mittens, hatband, nose)

9″ × 12″ black (hat, buttons)

6″ × 6″ green (scarf)

2″ × 6″ purple (earmuffs)

For Santa:

9″ × 12″ white (pom-pom, trim, beard, mustache, eyebrows)

6″ × 9″ pink (face)

scraps of red for nose and black for eyes

X-acto knife

Ruler

Red chalk

Red poster paint and brush (Santa)

Liquid soap (Santa)

Two plastic eyes (optional)

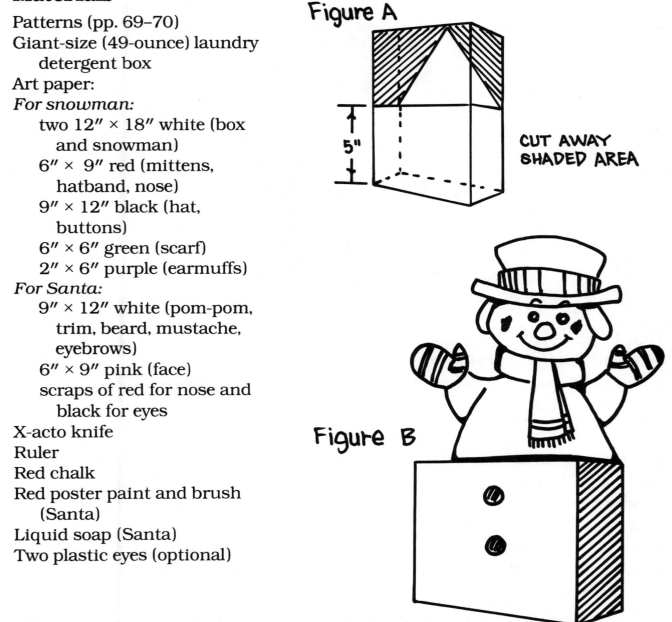

Figure A

CUT AWAY SHADED AREA

5″

Figure B

Holiday Gifts and Decorations, © 1986

Procedure

For snowman:

1. Measure and cut top portion of box using ruler and X-acto knife (fig. A).
2. Cover remaining box with white art paper. Glue paper in place.
3. Trace patterns on art paper and cut out.

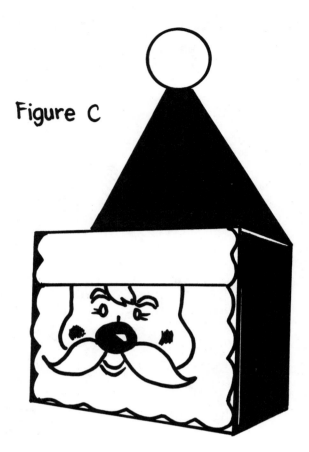

Figure C

4. Glue head and arms in place first. Follow with earmuffs, hat, hatband, scarf, mittens, and buttons (fig. B).

5. Glue on nose and eyes. Draw mouth and eyebrows with black felt pen.

6. Rub red chalk on cheeks with finger.

For Santa:

1. Cut top portion of box as shown (fig. A).

2. Add one teaspoon of liquid soap to poster paint. (The soap helps paint to adhere to box.) Paint box. Allow to dry.

3. Glue pink paper to front of box for face (fig. C).

4. Trace patterns for beard, hat band, pom-pom, and mustache on white paper. Cut out and glue in place (fig. C).

5. Cut out eyes and nose from scraps of paper and glue on face.

6. Rub red chalk on cheeks with finger.

68

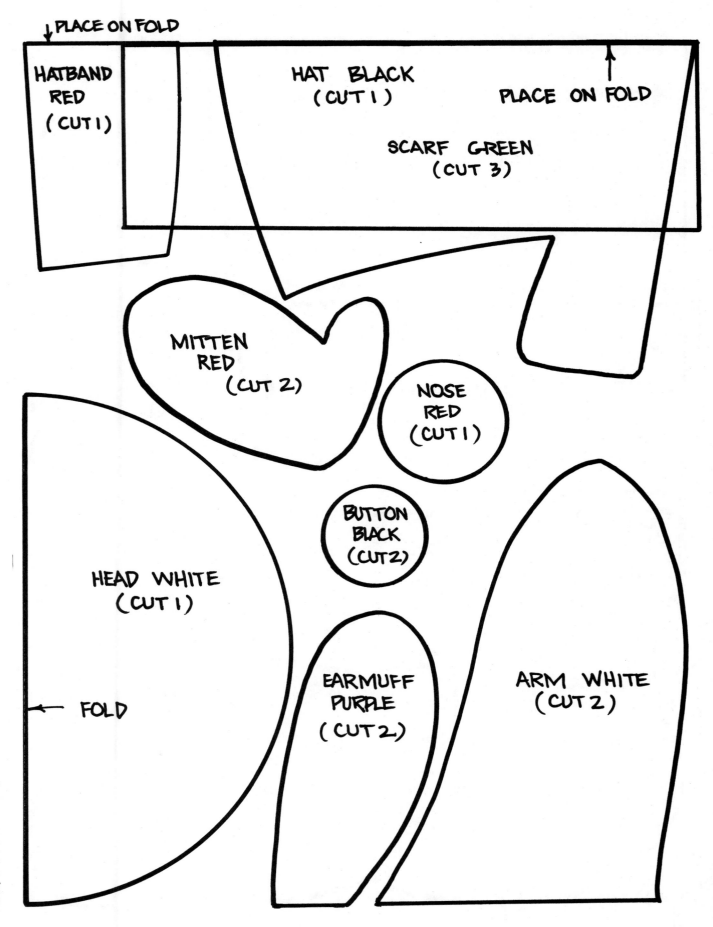

PLACE ON FOLD

HATBAND
RED
(CUT 1)

HAT BLACK
(CUT 1)

PLACE ON FOLD

SCARF GREEN
(CUT 3)

MITTEN
RED
(CUT 2)

NOSE
RED
(CUT 1)

BUTTON
BLACK
(CUT 2)

HEAD WHITE
(CUT 1)

ARM WHITE
(CUT 2)

FOLD

EARMUFF
PURPLE
(CUT 2)

PLACE ON FOLD

FACE PINK
(CUT 1)

NOSE RED
(CUT 1)

PLACE
ON
FOLD

HATBAND WHITE
(CUT 1)

BEARD WHITE
(CUT 1)

PLACE ON
FOLD

MUSTACHE WHITE
(CUT 1)

WHITE
POM - POM
(CUT 1)

PLACE ON
FOLD

Egg Carton Ornaments

Materials

Paper egg carton for each
    ornament
Stapler
Hole punch
Paper clip
Poster paint and brush or
    spray paint
Yarn
Small Christmas balls

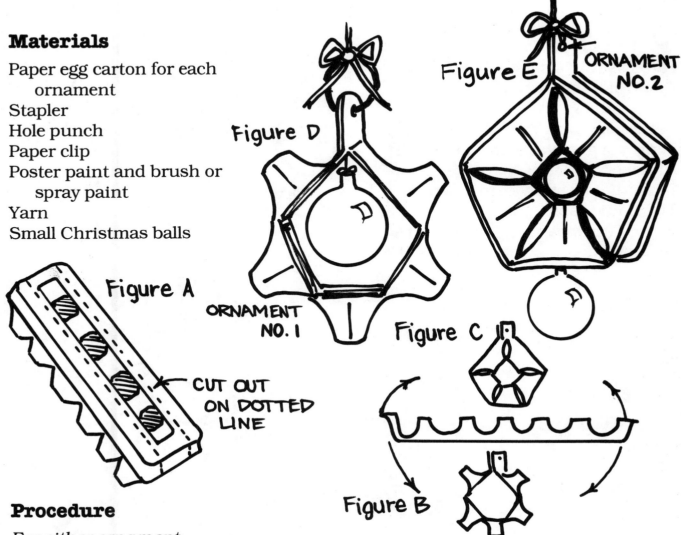

Figure D

Figure E

ORNAMENT NO.2

Figure A

ORNAMENT NO. 1

CUT OUT ON DOTTED LINE

Figure C

Figure B

Procedure

For either ornament:

1. Cut top portion of egg carton as shown, saving only the center section (fig. A).
2. Bend cut-out portion and staple ends together (fig. B or C).
3. Spray paint or brush on poster paint. Allow to dry.

For ornament No. 1:

4. Hang Christmas ball in center of ornament by inserting opened paper clip through top of ornament and attaching Christmas ball (fig. D). Bend other end of paper clip for hanging. Tie one yarn bow to top of center ball and another yarn bow to end of paper clip hanger (fig. D).

For ornament No. 2:

4. Punch hole in top of ornament and thread 6″ length of yarn through. Tie into bow. Glue Christmas ball in center of ornament and hang one from bottom (fig. E).

Holiday Gifts and Decorations, © 1986

Stocking Container Candle Holders

Materials

Patterns (this page)
Two plastic egg stocking
    containers
Bathroom paper roll
Scraps of green and gold art
    paper
Silver or gold spray paint
Two bottle caps
5″ × 6″ cardboard
Green yarn

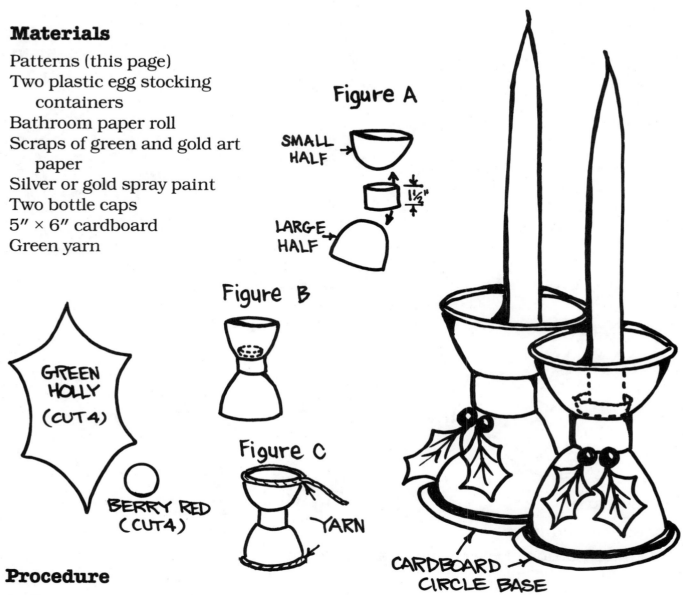

Figure A

SMALL HALF

1½″

LARGE HALF

Figure B

Figure C

GREEN HOLLY (CUT 4)

BERRY RED (CUT 4)

YARN

CARDBOARD CIRCLE BASE

Procedure

1. Cut two 1½″-long pieces from paper roll.
2. Glue paper roll between halves of plastic egg as shown (fig. A).
3. Glue bottle cap in bottom of small egg half (fig. B).
4. Repeat steps 2 and 3 for second candle holder.
5. Trace and cut out two cardboard circles using the rim of large half of plastic egg as a pattern. Glue one circle to bottom of each large egg half for base. Allow to dry.
6. Spray holders with silver or gold paint. Allow to dry.
7. Trace and cut holly and berries from art paper. Glue in place.
8. Cut yarn to fit and glue around top lid and base of each candle holder (fig. C).

Holiday Gifts and Decorations, © 1986

Santa Coffee Can Cookie Jar

Materials

Patterns (p. 74)
Two-pound coffee can
Art paper:
    12″ × 18″ red (hat cone)
    6⅛″ × 18″ red (can)
    2″ × 18″ white (hat trim)
    12″ × 18″ white (beard,
      mustache, eyebrows,
      pom-pom)
    5″ × 5″ pink (face)
    4″ × 4″ green (holly)
Stapler
Three pipe cleaners
Small red ornament (nose)
Red chalk (cheeks)
Two plastic eyes (optional)

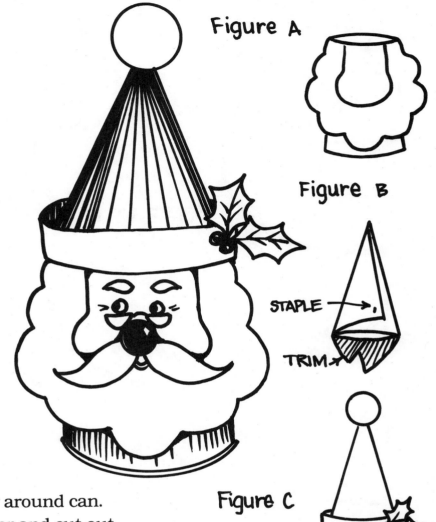

Figure A

Figure B

Figure C

Procedure

1. Glue 6⅛″ × 18″ red paper around can.
2. Trace patterns on art paper and cut out.
3. Glue face to can.
4. Apply glue along inside edge of beard and place on face (fig. A).
5. Glue on mustache, ornament nose, plastic or paper eyes, and eyebrows.
6. Rub red chalk on cheeks with finger.
7. Roll 12″ × 18″ red paper into cone. Staple and trim to fit can (fig. B).
8. Staple 2″ × 18″ white paper around bottom of cone for trim. Glue on pom-pom (fig. C).
9. Staple holly in place (fig. C). Place hat on can.
10. Shape eyeglasses from pipe cleaners (fig. D) and place on nose.

Figure D

Holiday Gifts and Decorations, © 1986

73

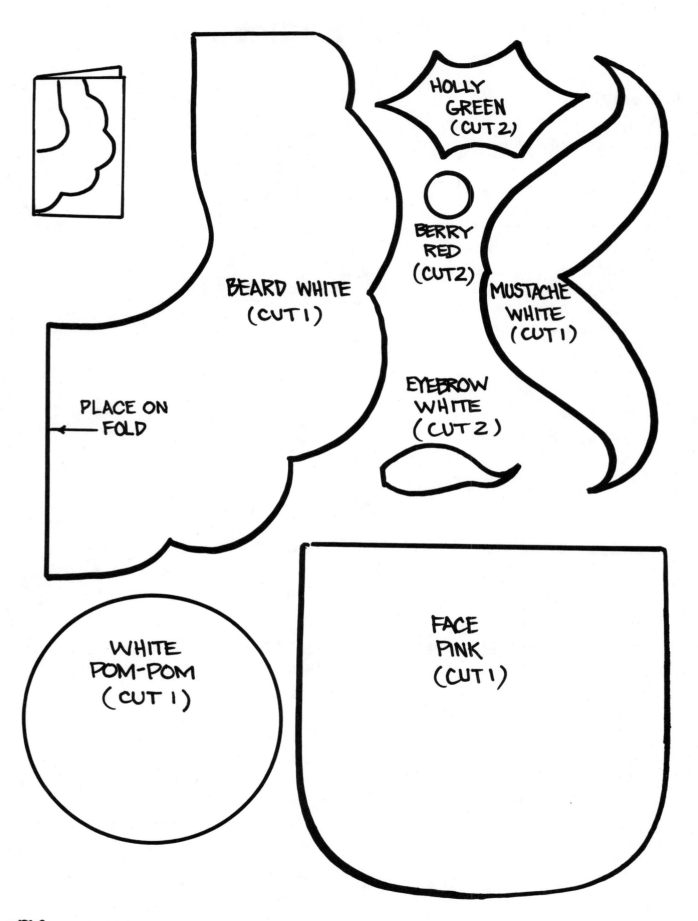

HOLLY
GREEN
(CUT 2)

BERRY
RED
(CUT 2)

MUSTACHE
WHITE
(CUT 1)

BEARD WHITE
(CUT 1)

EYEBROW
WHITE
(CUT 2)

PLACE ON
← FOLD

WHITE
POM-POM
(CUT 1)

FACE
PINK
(CUT 1)

Snowman Coffee Can Cookie Jar

Materials

Patterns (p. 76)
Two-pound coffee can
Art paper:
    6⅛″ × 18″ white (can)
    4″ × 5″ green (holly)
    5″ × 9″ red (earmuffs,
      berries, nose)
    1½″ × 4″ black (tabs)
    1½″ × 12″ red (hatband)
    1½″ × 18″ blue (scarf)
    1½″ × 6″ blue (scarf tails)
    5″ × 12″ black (hat)
    two 7″ × 7″ black (brim)
7″ × 7″ tagboard
½″ × 1″ piece of sponge (pipe)
2″ length of pipe cleaner
Two plastic eyes (optional)

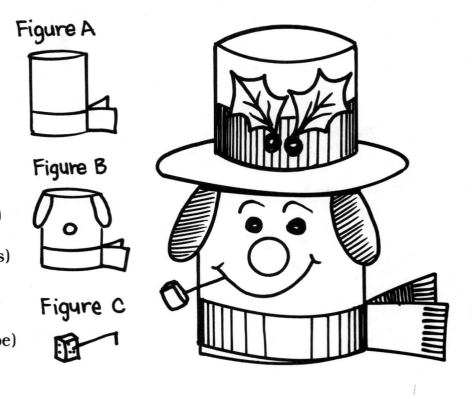

Figure A

Figure B

Figure C

Procedure

1. Glue 6⅛″ × 18″ white paper around can.
2. Glue 1½″ × 18″ blue paper around base of can for scarf. Fold 1½″ × 6″ blue paper in half and glue or staple in place for scarf tails (fig. A).
3. Trace earmuffs and nose on red paper and cut out. Glue in place (fig. B).
4. Glue on plastic or art-paper eyes.
5. Draw eyebrows and mouth with black felt pen.
6. Poke hole in sponge with scissors. Put glue on tip of pipe cleaner and insert in hole. Bend other end of pipe cleaner (fig. C). Poke hole in mouth, put glue on bent end of pipe cleaner, and insert in mouth for pipe.
7. Roll 5″ × 12″ black paper into cylinder for hat. Overlap edges about ¼″ and staple. Glue on four tabs as shown on page 76 (fig. D).
8. Trace hat brim pattern on black paper and cut out two.
9. Glue the two circles together with tagboard in between (fig. E). Trim tagboard.
10. Glue black cylinder to black circles with tabs (fig. F).
11. Glue on 1½″ red strip for hatband. Trace holly and berries, cut out, and glue to hatband (fig. D).

Holiday Gifts and Decorations, © 1986

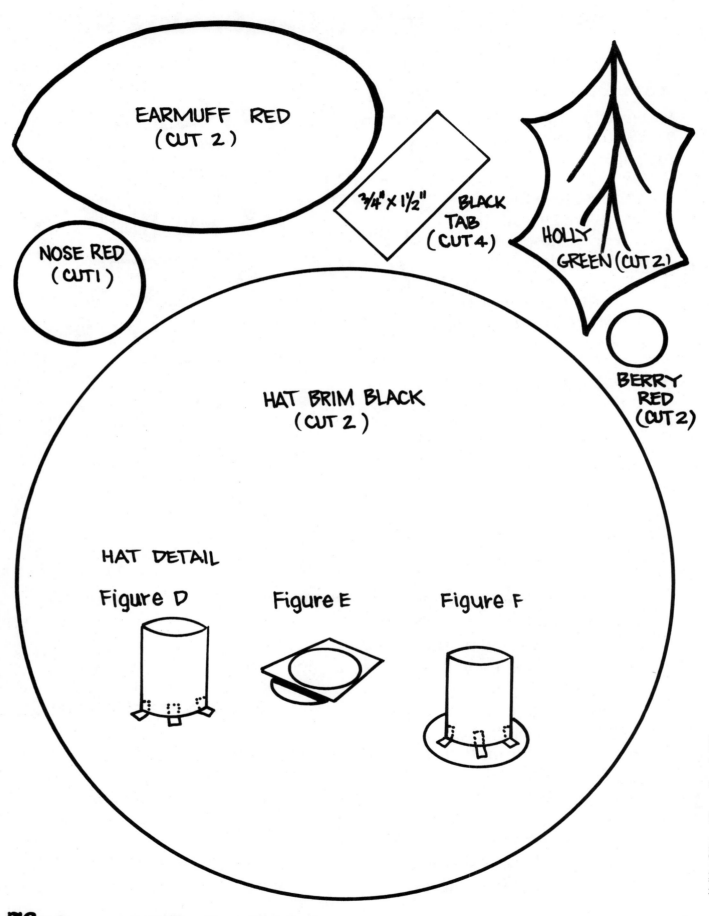

EARMUFF RED
(CUT 2)

NOSE RED
(CUT 1)

3/4" x 1½"   BLACK TAB
(CUT 4)

HOLLY GREEN (CUT 2)

BERRY RED
(CUT 2)

HAT BRIM BLACK
(CUT 2)

HAT DETAIL

Figure D   Figure E   Figure F

Angel and Candle Paper Plate Hang-Ups

Materials

Patterns (p. 78)
Two 7″ red paper plates
Art paper:
> 8″ × 8″ white (candle glow,
>   angel, wings)
> 4″ × 4½″ yellow (candle,
>   halo)
> 5″ × 6″ black (candle
>   holder, hair)
> 2″ × 2″ red (flame)

2″ × 2″ tagboard (hanger)
Three yards green yarn
Hole punch
Hair spray
Gold or silver glitter

Figure A

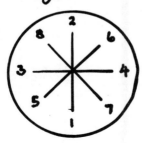

Figure B

Procedure

1. Punch eight equally spaced holes around each plate, one inch from edge (fig. A).
2. Thread yarn through holes once around plate. Repeat in opposite direction and tie a bow at bottom to finish (fig. B).
3. Trace patterns on art paper and cut out. Assemble and glue in place as shown.
4. Spray plates with hair spray and sprinkle with glitter.
5. Trace hanger pattern on tagboard and cut out two. Glue one to back of each plate.

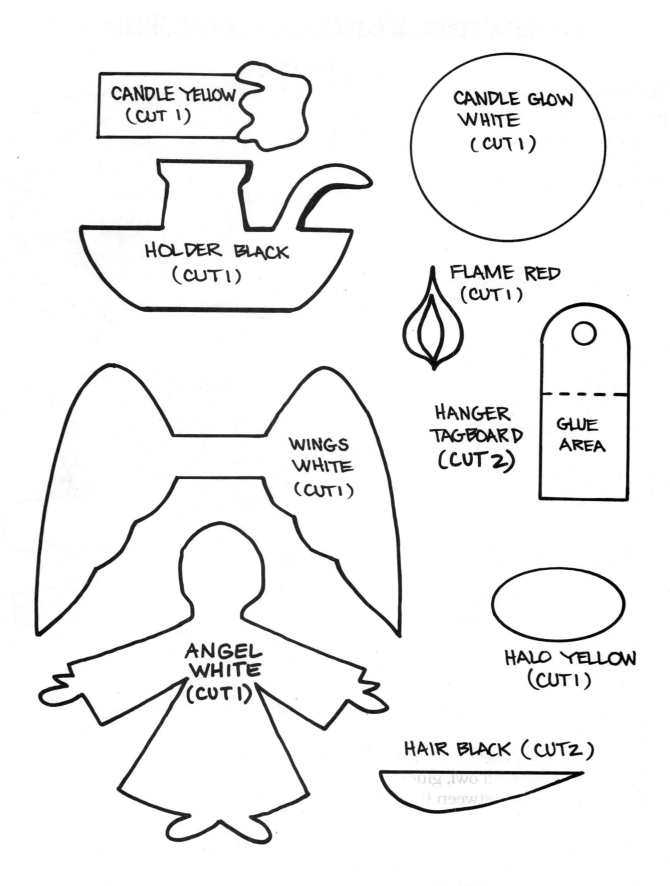

CANDLE YELLOW
(CUT 1)

CANDLE GLOW
WHITE
(CUT 1)

HOLDER BLACK
(CUT 1)

FLAME RED
(CUT 1)

WINGS
WHITE
(CUT 1)

HANGER
TAGBOARD
(CUT 2)

GLUE
AREA

ANGEL
WHITE
(CUT 1)

HALO YELLOW
(CUT 1)

HAIR BLACK (CUT 2)

Holiday Gifts and Decorations, © 1986

Walnut Shell Ornaments

Materials

Patterns (p. 80)
Two walnut shell halves for
     each ornament
Art paper of various colors
Poster paints of various colors
Brush
Thread
Plastic eyes (optional)
Cotton balls (Santa's beard)

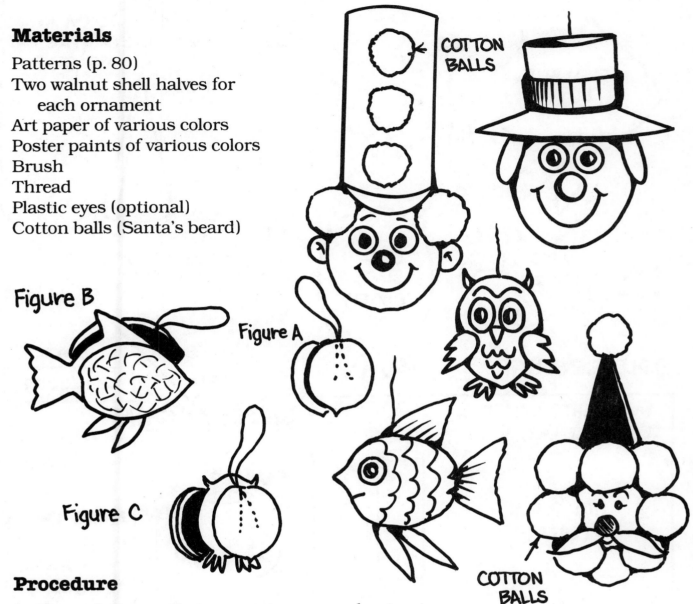

Figure B

Figure A

Figure C

COTTON BALLS

COTTON BALLS

Procedure

1. Trace chosen patterns on art paper and cut out.
2. Paint walnut shells according to pattern chosen—Santa and soldier, pink; fish and snowman, white; owl, natural or brown. Allow to dry.
3. Cut a ten-inch piece of thread and make a loop (fig. A).
4. Glue two walnut halves together with ends of thread loop in between (fig. A). For fish and owl, glue walnut halves together with thread and body patterns in between (figs. B and C).
5. Glue other pattern pieces to shell as shown, following instructions that accompany patterns. For Santa, glue on cotton balls for beard.
6. Glue plastic or art-paper eyes in place.
7. Draw other details with black felt pen.

Holiday Gifts and Decorations, © 1986

79

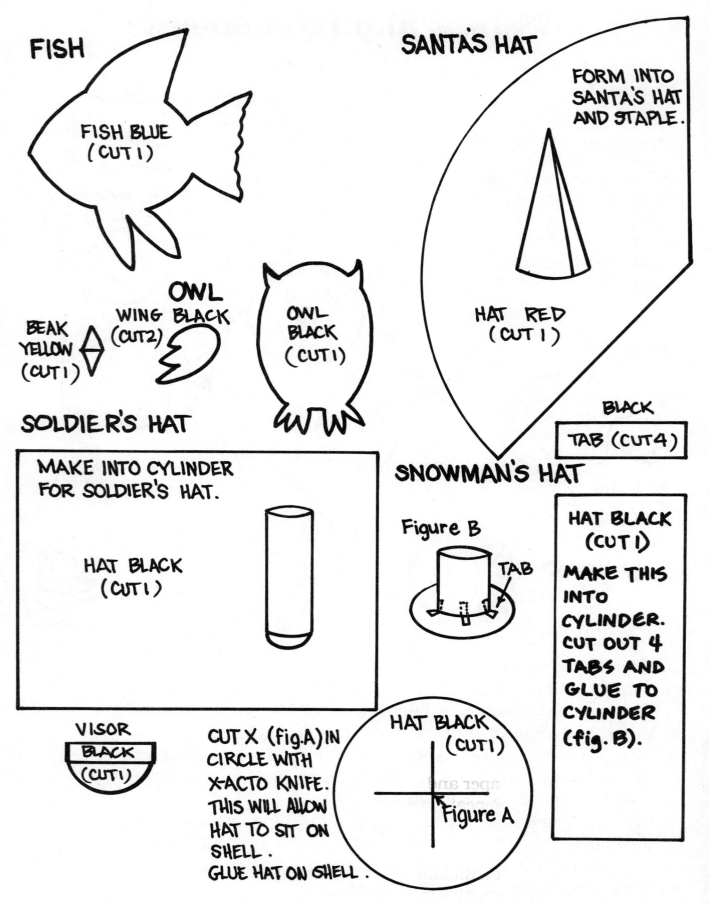

FISH

FISH BLUE
(CUT 1)

SANTA'S HAT

FORM INTO
SANTA'S HAT
AND STAPLE.

HAT RED
(CUT 1)

OWL

BEAK
YELLOW
(CUT 1)

WING BLACK
(CUT 2)

OWL
BLACK
(CUT 1)

BLACK

TAB (CUT 4)

SOLDIER'S HAT

MAKE INTO CYLINDER
FOR SOLDIER'S HAT.

HAT BLACK
(CUT 1)

SNOWMAN'S HAT

Figure B

TAB

HAT BLACK
(CUT 1)

MAKE THIS
INTO
CYLINDER.
CUT OUT 4
TABS AND
GLUE TO
CYLINDER
(fig. B).

VISOR
BLACK
(CUT 1)

CUT X (fig. A) IN
CIRCLE WITH
X-ACTO KNIFE.
THIS WILL ALLOW
HAT TO SIT ON
SHELL.
GLUE HAT ON SHELL.

HAT BLACK
(CUT 1)

Figure A

Paper Roll Ornaments

Materials

Bathroom paper roll
Art paper:
>   9″ × 12″ red (drum, Santa's
>   hat, snowman's earmuff)
>   9″ × 12″ black (drum trim,
>   snowman's hat)
>   2¼″ × 6″ pink (Santa)
>   2¼″ × 6″ white (snowman)
>   scraps of yellow and green
>   (snowman's scarf and
>   hatband)

X-acto knife
Cotton balls (Santa)
10″ length of yarn
Glitter
Small red beads (noses)
Two wood matches
Gold paint and brush

Figure A

Figure B

GLUE AROUND OPENING

PRESS DOWN ON PAPER. ALLOW TO DRY.

TRIM EDGES.

Procedure

For drum:

1. With X-acto knife, cut paper roll in half.
2. Cut a 2¼″ × 5½″ strip of red paper and glue around paper roll (fig. A).
3. Apply glue around opening at one end of roll. Press end down on 2″ × 2″ piece of black paper and allow to dry. Turn edges up to make trim as shown (fig. B). Repeat with other end.
4. Punch hole ⅛″ from one edge of roll and thread yarn through. Tie ends.
5. Draw details with black felt pen.
6. Apply glue to black trim and sprinkle with glitter.
7. Paint two matches gold and allow to dry. Glue to top of drum.

Holiday Gifts and Decorations, © 1986

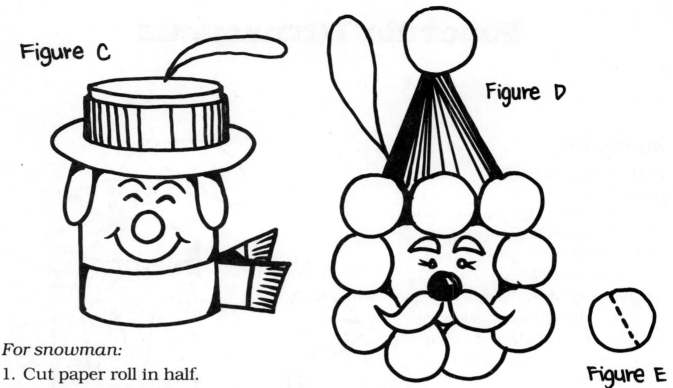

Figure C

Figure D

Figure E

For snowman:

1. Cut paper roll in half.
2. Glue a 2¼″ × 5½″ strip of white paper around paper roll.
3. Punch a hole ⅛″ in from one edge of roll and thread yarn through. Tie ends.
4. Apply glue around opening at opposite end of roll. Press end of roll down on 2″ × 2″ piece of black paper and allow to dry. Trim edges.
5. Cut out a ¾″ × 5½″ strip of black paper for hat. Glue it around end of paper roll that has black circle attached. Cut out a 2⅝″-diameter circle from black paper. Cut out the inside of this circle to slip over top of paper roll for hat brim (fig. C). Glue in place.
6. Cut out a ¼″ × 5½″ strip of green paper for scarf. Glue it around bottom of paper roll, extending and cutting for scarf fringe.
7. Draw facial features with black felt pen.
8. Glue on small red bead for nose.

For Santa:

1. Cut paper roll in half.
2. Glue a 2¼″ × 5½″ strip of pink paper around paper roll.
3. Punch hole ⅛″ from one edge of roll and thread yarn through. Tie ends.
4. Make cone hat from 4½″ × 6″ red paper. Staple ends, trim off excess, and glue in place (fig. D).
5. Cut cotton balls in half for hat trim and beard. Glue in place (fig. D).
6. Cut a cotton ball in half (fig. E) and shape for mustache. Glue in place.
7. Draw eyes and eyebrows with felt pen.
8. Glue on small red bead for nose.

82

Holiday Gifts and Decorations, © 1986

Doorknob Decorations

Materials

Patterns (pp. 84–86)
Tagboard
9″ × 12″ art paper:
    red and green (Christmas)
    black and orange
      (Halloween)
    various colors for details

Figure A

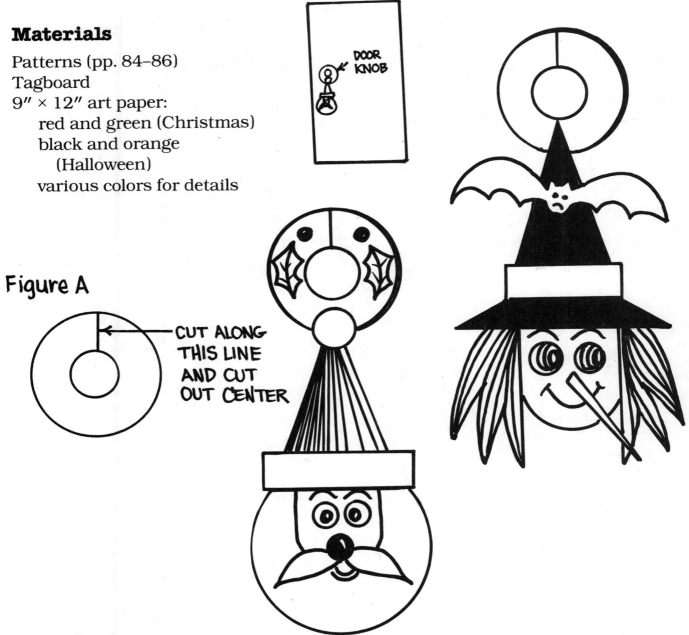

CUT ALONG THIS LINE AND CUT OUT CENTER

Procedure

1. Trace two hanger patterns on art paper.
2. Glue art paper to tagboard and cut out along lines.
3. Make a cut from the edge of each hanger to the middle of the circle and then cut out the center (fig. A).
4. Trace detail patterns on art paper, cut out, and glue in place as shown.
5. Draw other details with black felt pen.

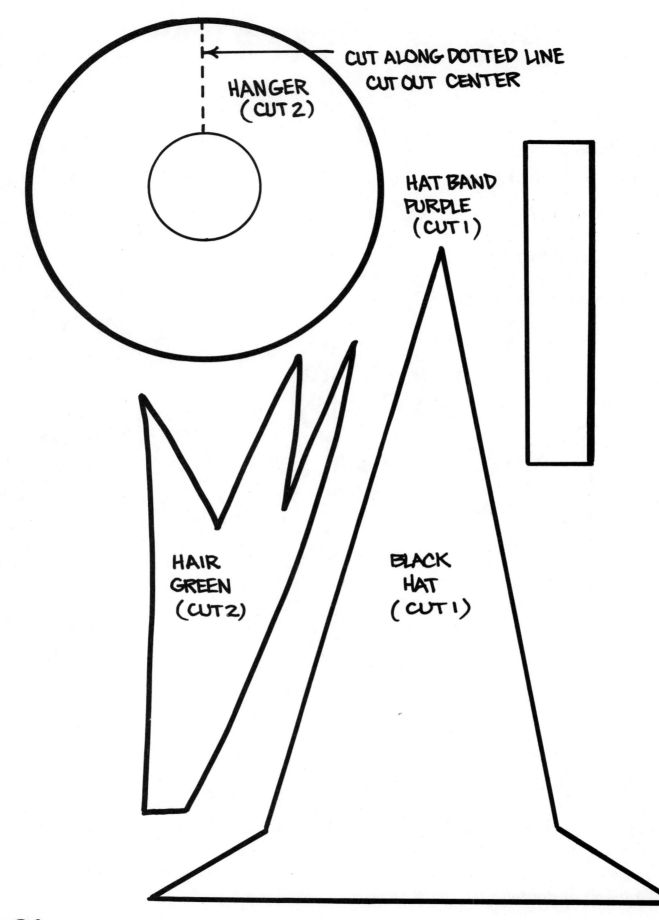

CUT ALONG DOTTED LINE
CUT OUT CENTER

HANGER
(CUT 2)

HAT BAND
PURPLE
(CUT 1)

HAIR
GREEN
(CUT 2)

BLACK
HAT
(CUT 1)

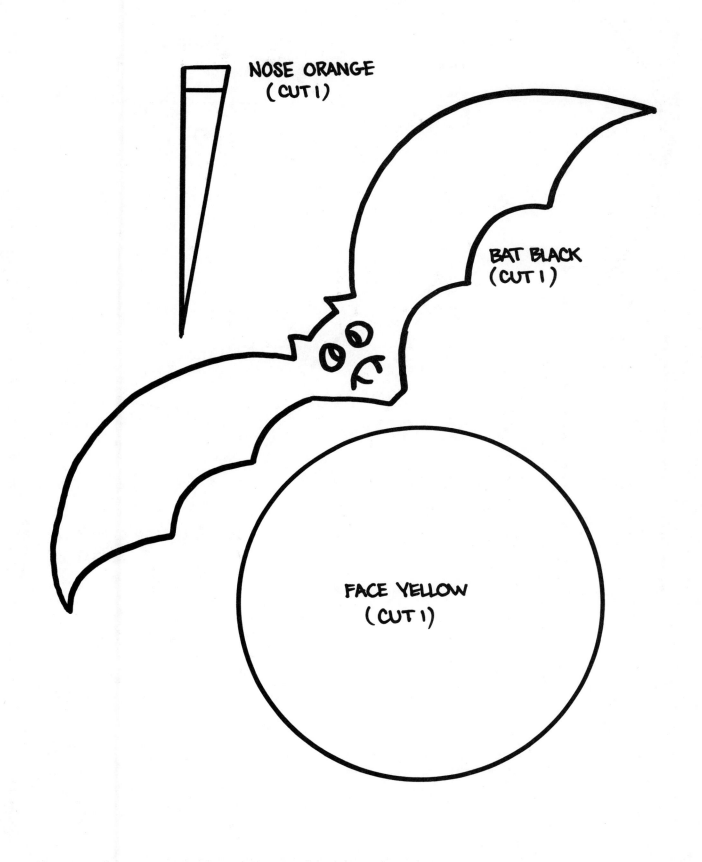

NOSE ORANGE
(CUT 1)

BAT BLACK
(CUT 1)

FACE YELLOW
(CUT 1)

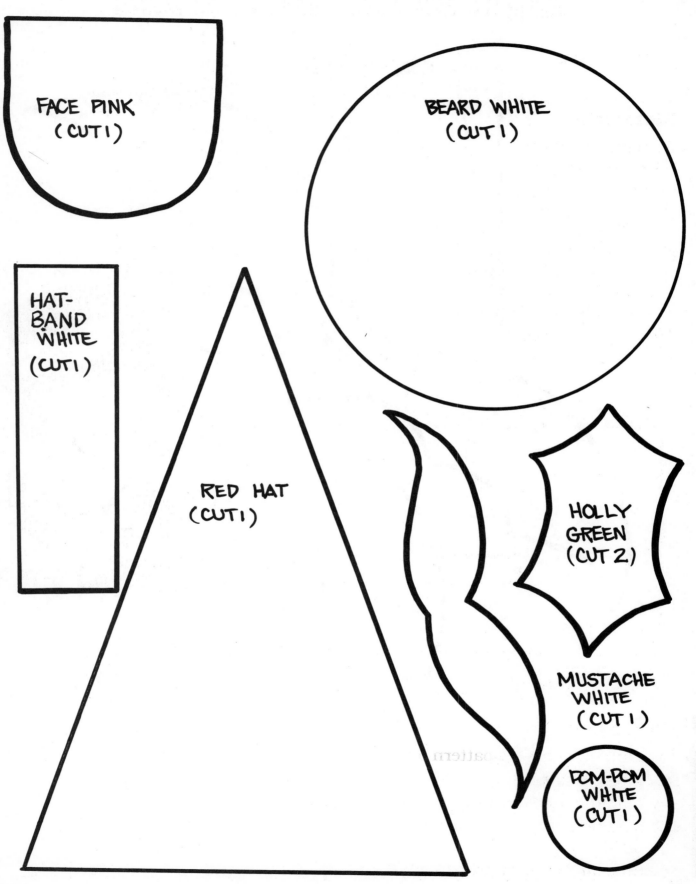

FACE PINK
(CUT 1)

BEARD WHITE
(CUT 1)

HAT-
BAND
WHITE
(CUT 1)

RED HAT
(CUT 1)

HOLLY
GREEN
(CUT 2)

MUSTACHE
WHITE
(CUT 1)

POM-POM
WHITE
(CUT 1)

Holiday Gifts and Decorations, © 1986

Light Switch Decorations

Materials

Patterns (pp. 88–90)

9″ × 12″ tagboard (makes six decorations)

9″ × 12″ art paper:
   red, green, pink, and white (Christmas)
   black, white, and orange (Halloween)
   various colors for details

Plastic eyes (optional)

Figure B

Figure C

Figure D

Figure A

Procedure

1. Trace light switch pattern on tagboard.
2. Cut out hole for light switch and screws to extend through (fig. A).
3. Trace detail patterns on art paper and cut out.
4. Assemble cutouts as shown and glue to light switch cover (fig. B, C, or D).
5. Glue on plastic or art-paper eyes.

Holiday Gifts and Decorations, © 1986

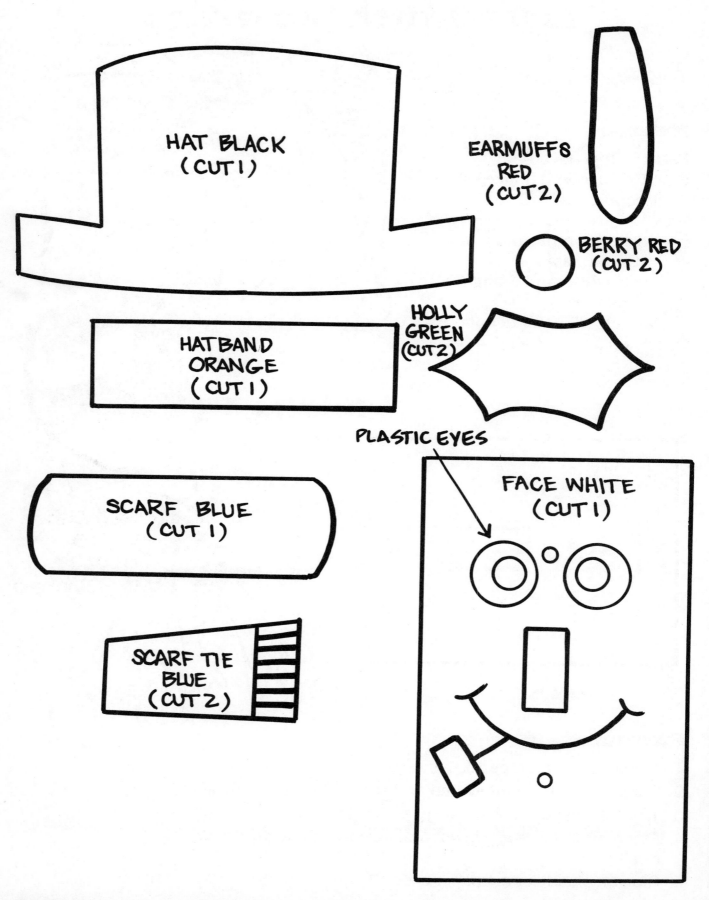

HAT BLACK
(CUT 1)

EARMUFFS
RED
(CUT 2)

BERRY RED
(CUT 2)

HATBAND
ORANGE
(CUT 1)

HOLLY
GREEN
(CUT 2)

PLASTIC EYES

FACE WHITE
(CUT 1)

SCARF BLUE
(CUT 1)

SCARF TIE
BLUE
(CUT 2)

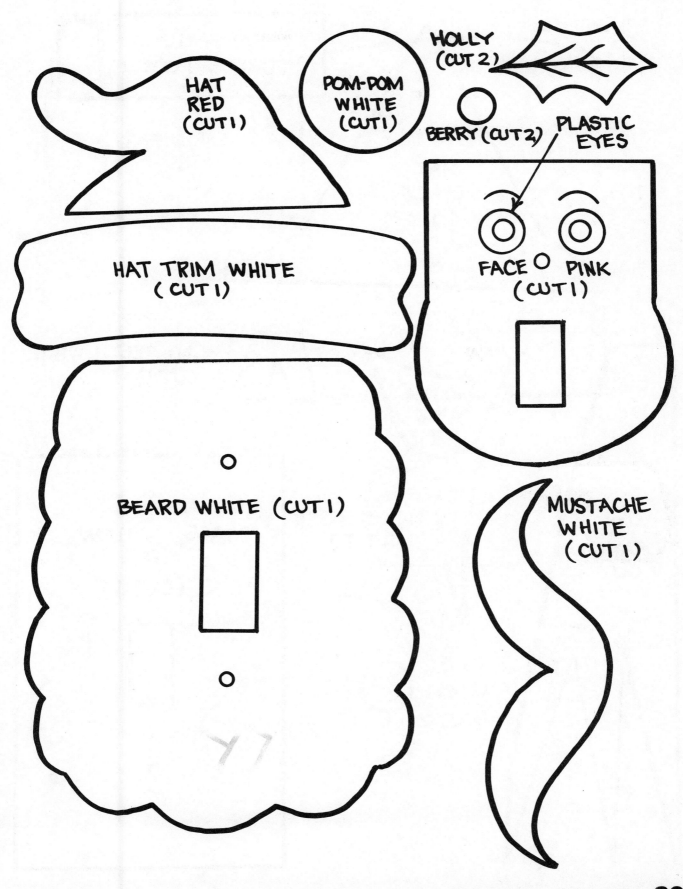

HAT
RED
(CUT 1)

POM-POM
WHITE
(CUT 1)

HOLLY
(CUT 2)

BERRY (CUT 2)

PLASTIC
EYES

HAT TRIM WHITE
(CUT 1)

FACE ○ PINK
(CUT 1)

BEARD WHITE (CUT 1)

MUSTACHE
WHITE
(CUT 1)

Holiday Gifts and Decorations, © 1986

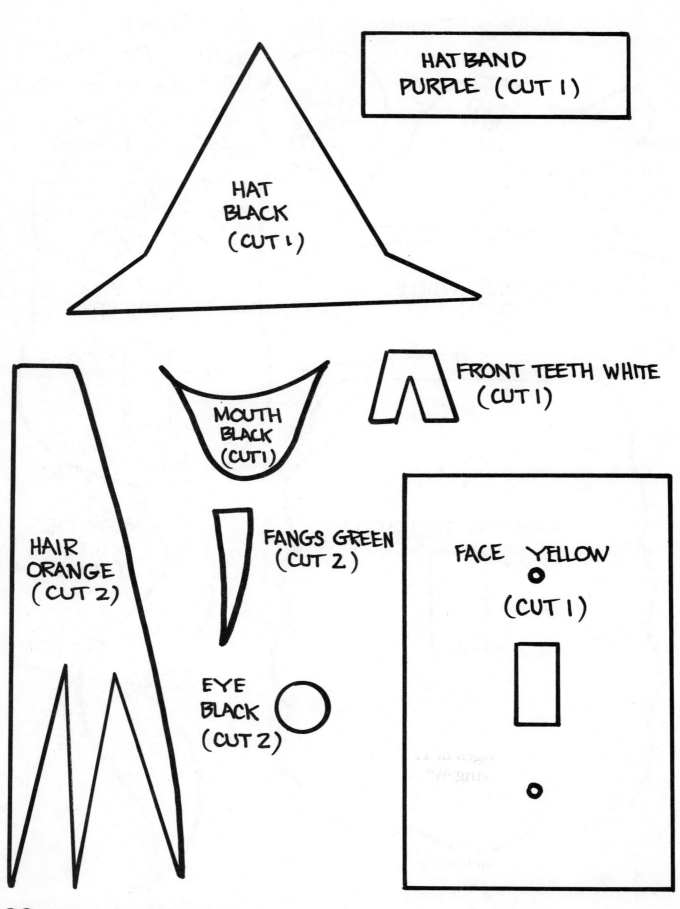

HATBAND
PURPLE (CUT 1)

HAT
BLACK
(CUT 1)

FRONT TEETH WHITE
(CUT 1)

MOUTH
BLACK
(CUT 1)

HAIR
ORANGE
(CUT 2)

FANGS GREEN
(CUT 2)

FACE YELLOW
(CUT 1)

EYE
BLACK
(CUT 2)

Holiday Gifts and Decorations, © 1986

Wire Hanger Decorations

Materials

Patterns (pp. 92–94)
Wire hanger
12″ × 18″ art paper of any
    color
Assorted scraps of art paper
Colored plastic tape

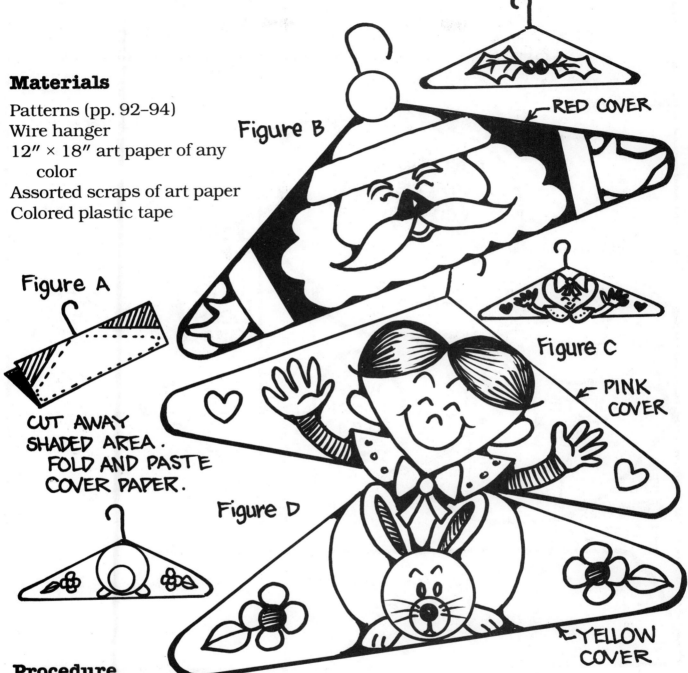

Figure B

RED COVER

Figure A

CUT AWAY
SHADED AREA.
FOLD AND PASTE
COVER PAPER.

Figure C

PINK COVER

Figure D

YELLOW COVER

Procedure

1. Fold together long edges of 12″ × 18″ art paper. Insert hanger. Trim off corners of paper, leaving ¾″-wide flaps (fig. A). Fold flaps over hanger and glue on back (fig. A).
2. Trace chosen patterns on colored art paper and cut out.
3. Assemble the cutouts and glue on hanger as shown (figs. B, C, or D).
4. Draw details with black felt pen.
5. Cover hook of hanger with colored tape.

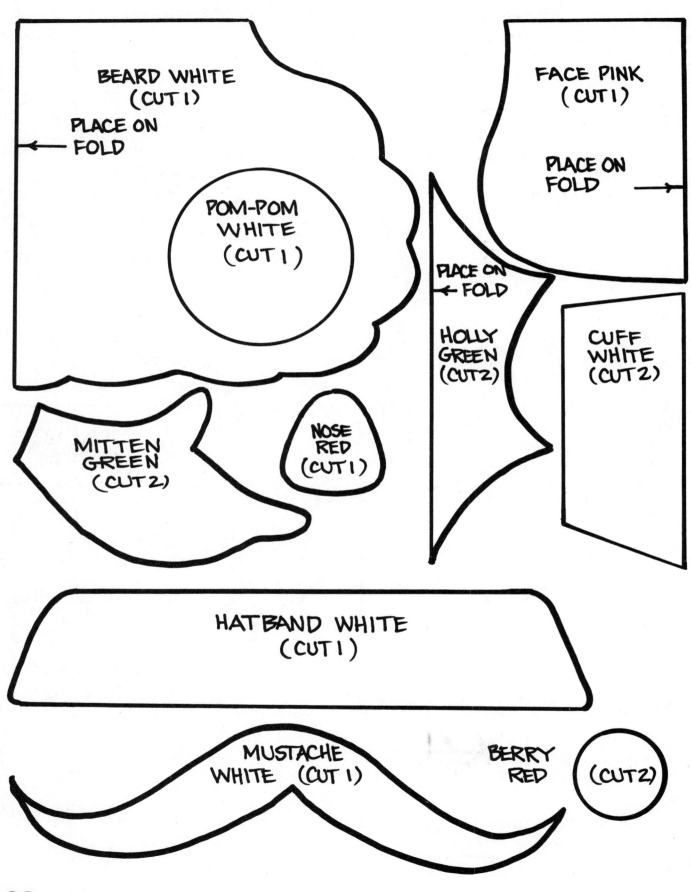

BEARD WHITE
(CUT 1)

PLACE ON
FOLD

POM-POM
WHITE
(CUT 1)

FACE PINK
(CUT 1)

PLACE ON
FOLD

PLACE ON
FOLD

HOLLY
GREEN
(CUT 2)

CUFF
WHITE
(CUT 2)

MITTEN
GREEN
(CUT 2)

NOSE
RED
(CUT 1)

HATBAND WHITE
(CUT 1)

MUSTACHE
WHITE (CUT 1)

BERRY
RED

(CUT 2)

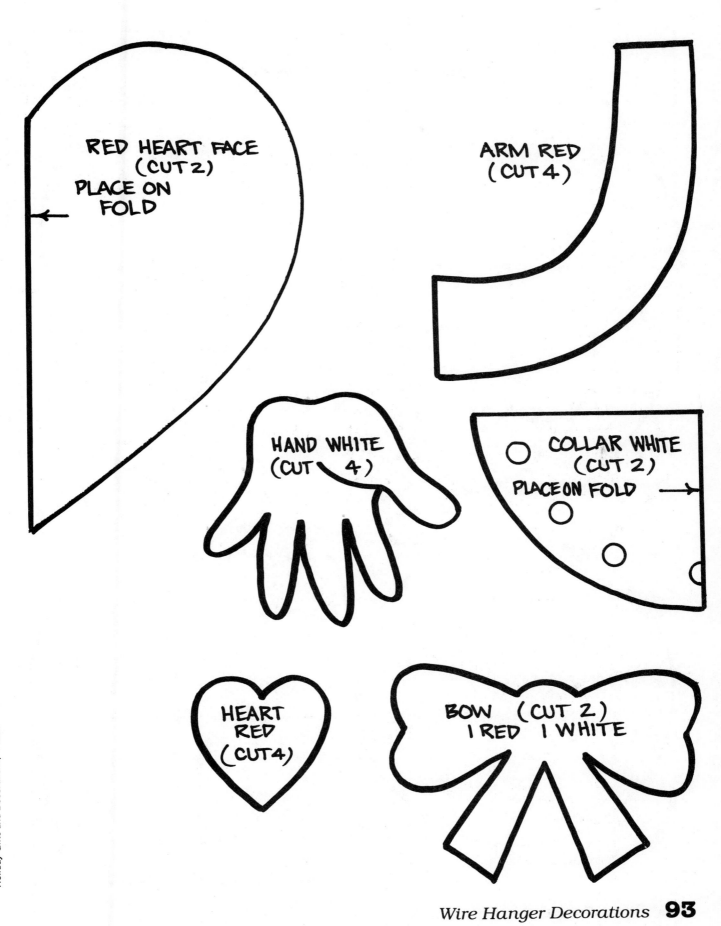

RED HEART FACE
(CUT 2)
PLACE ON
FOLD

ARM RED
(CUT 4)

HAND WHITE
(CUT 4)

COLLAR WHITE
(CUT 2)
PLACE ON FOLD

HEART
RED
(CUT 4)

BOW (CUT 2)
1 RED 1 WHITE

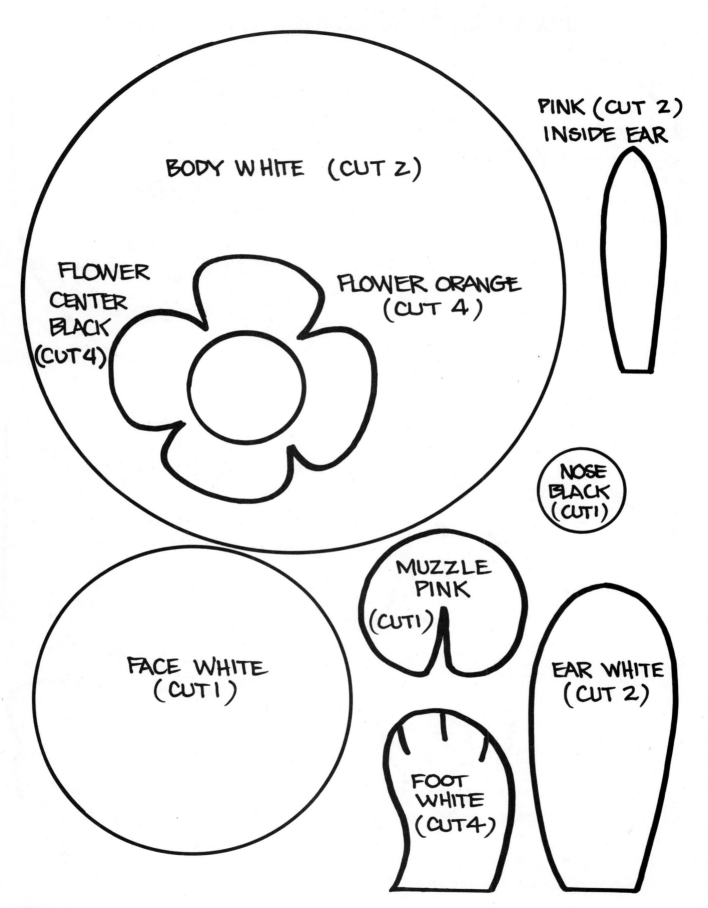

BODY WHITE (CUT 2)

PINK (CUT 2)
INSIDE EAR

FLOWER
CENTER
BLACK
(CUT 4)

FLOWER ORANGE
(CUT 4)

NOSE
BLACK
(CUT 1)

MUZZLE
PINK
(CUT 1)

FACE WHITE
(CUT 1)

EAR WHITE
(CUT 2)

FOOT
WHITE
(CUT 4)

Tuna Can Holiday Coaster

Materials

Pattern (this page)
Art paper:
    1½″ × 12″ red (can)
    4″ × 5″ green (holly)
    4″ × 5″ red or green
      (bottom of can)
¼″-diameter red Christmas
    beads (holly berries)
Spray lacquer
Glitter

GREEN HOLLY

(CUT 4)

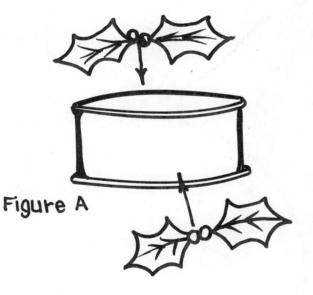

Figure A

Procedure

1. Glue 1½″ × 12″ red paper around can.
2. Trace circle on red or green paper using can as pattern. Cut out and glue to inside bottom of can.
3. Trace holly pattern on green paper and cut out four leaves.
4. Glue two holly leaves and two red beads on two opposite sides of can (fig. A).
5. Spray can with lacquer for water resistance.
6. Sprinkle holly with glitter while lacquer is still wet.

Clothespin Snap-Ons

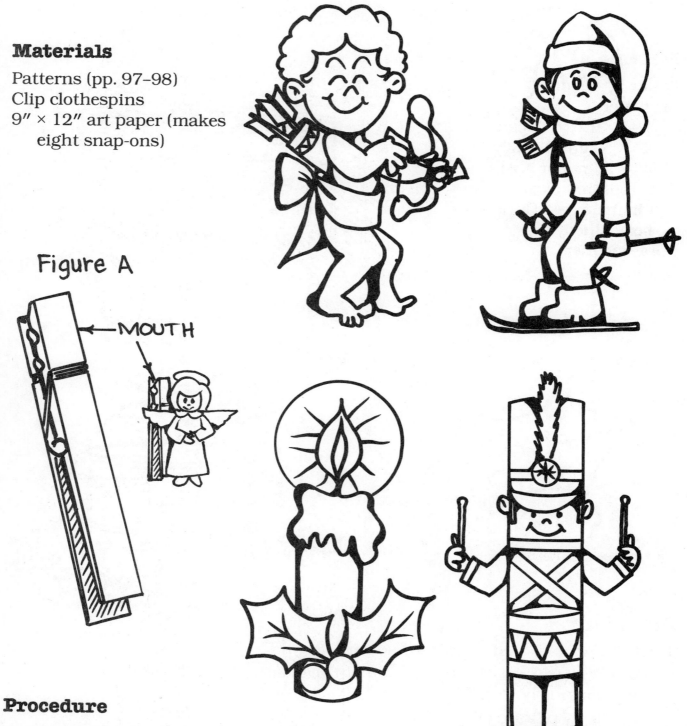

Materials

Patterns (pp. 97–98)
Clip clothespins
9″ × 12″ art paper (makes
   eight snap-ons)

Figure A

MOUTH

Procedure

1. Trace desired pattern on art paper.
2. Color with crayons or felt pens.
3. Cut out and glue to clothespin. Make sure mouth of clothespin is at
   top of the cutout (fig. A).

96

Napkin Holders or Place Cards

Materials

Patterns (pp. 100–101)
Art paper:
For Santa:
    three 6″ × 9″ white (beard,
      mustache, pom-pom)
    2″ × 7″ pink (face)
    three 4½″ × 12″ red
      (holders)
    1″ × 3″ red (nose)
For clown:
    three 4½″ × 12″ yellow
      (holders)
    three 3″ × 5″ pink (face)
    2″ × 9″ purple (hat)
    3″ × 4″ blue (tie)
    3″ × 3″ yellow (hatband)
    3″ × 6″ white (flower)
    3″ × 5″ red (mouth, nose)
Six 4½″ × 12″ pieces of
    tagboard
Plastic eyes (optional)
Small red ornaments (optional)
Cotton balls (optional)

PRINT NAME

PRINT NAME

Procedure

1. Trace three napkin holder or place card patterns on 4½″ × 12″ art paper.
2. Glue 4½″ × 12″ art paper to 4½″ × 12″ tagboard, cut out, fold where shown, and glue.
3. Choose holiday decoration patterns and trace them on art paper. Cut out and assemble on holders or place cards. Glue in place.
4. Draw details with crayons or felt pens.
5. Cotton balls may be used for Santa trim and small red ornaments for noses.
6. Glue on plastic or art-paper eyes.

Note: If you wish, patterns can be traced on white paper and colored with crayons or felt pens.

Holiday Gifts and Decorations, © 1986

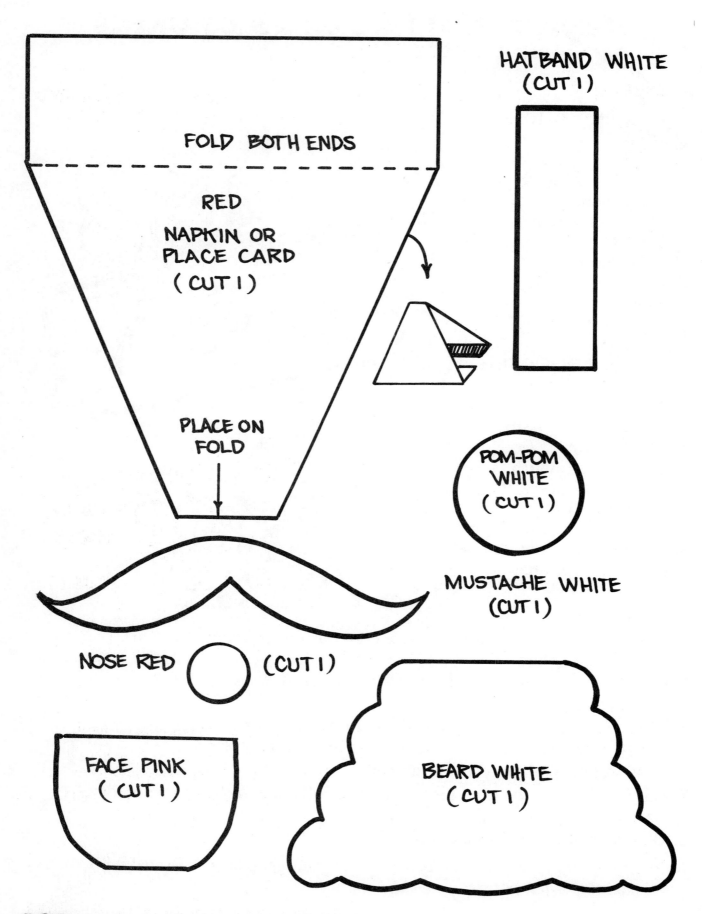

HATBAND WHITE
(CUT 1)

FOLD BOTH ENDS

RED

NAPKIN OR
PLACE CARD
(CUT 1)

PLACE ON
FOLD

POM-POM
WHITE
(CUT 1)

MUSTACHE WHITE
(CUT 1)

NOSE RED   (CUT 1)

FACE PINK
(CUT 1)

BEARD WHITE
(CUT 1)

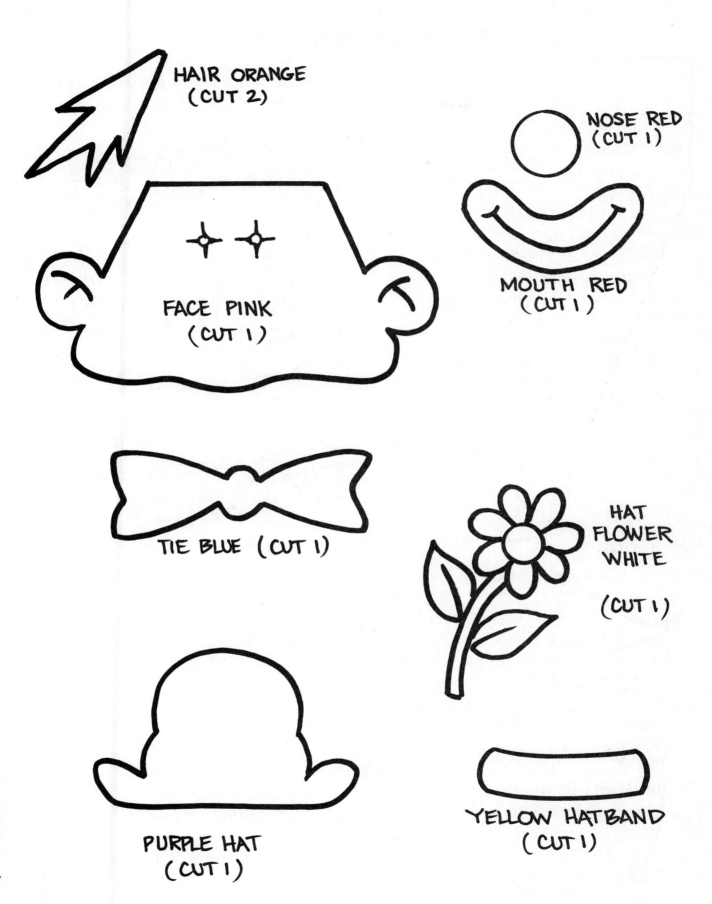

HAIR ORANGE
(CUT 2)

NOSE RED
(CUT 1)

MOUTH RED
(CUT 1)

FACE PINK
(CUT 1)

TIE BLUE (CUT 1)

HAT
FLOWER
WHITE

(CUT 1)

PURPLE HAT
(CUT 1)

YELLOW HATBAND
(CUT 1)

Hanukkah Wall Hanging

Materials

Patterns (p. 104)
Art paper:
    12″ × 18″ salmon
      (background)
    two 9″ ×12″ blue (menorah
      base, candle holders)
    12″ × 18″ white (candles)
    9″ × 12″ purple (trim,
      candle)
    4″ × 6″ red (flames)
    5″ × 12″ black (trim edges)
32″ length of yarn

Procedure

1. Cut black paper into two 2½″ × 12″ pieces. Fold each 2½″ × 12″ piece in half lengthwise.
2. Place yarn along inside fold of one piece and tie ends of yarn for hanging. Slip black paper over the top of salmon paper and glue in place for trim as shown on page 103 (fig. A). Slip other folded piece over bottom edge and glue.
3. Cut two ½″ × 12″ strips of purple paper. Glue them on salmon paper 2½″ from top and bottom edges (fig. A).
4. Trace menorah base pattern on blue paper and cut out. Fold out ¾″ along entire top edge. This fold will hold candles in place when finished (fig. B).
5. Center menorah base on salmon paper, 1½″ above bottom purple trim. Glue in place.
6. Cut eight 2¼″ × 6″ strips of blue paper for candle holders. Roll these strips into eight cylinders with ¾″ diameters. Glue edges together (fig. C).

7. Cut one 3¾″ × 4½″ strip of blue paper for center candle holder. Roll into ¾″-diameter cylinder and glue edges together (fig. C).

8. Glue nine candle holders in place on menorah.

9. Cut eight 3¾″ × 4½″ strips of white paper for candles. Cut one 4½″ × 5¼″ piece of purple paper for center candle. Roll into ½″-diameter cylinders and glue edges together. Insert candles into holders. The folded edge of the menorah base will prevent them from falling through (fig. D).

10. Trace flame pattern on red paper and cut out nine. Glue to insides of candles (fig. E).

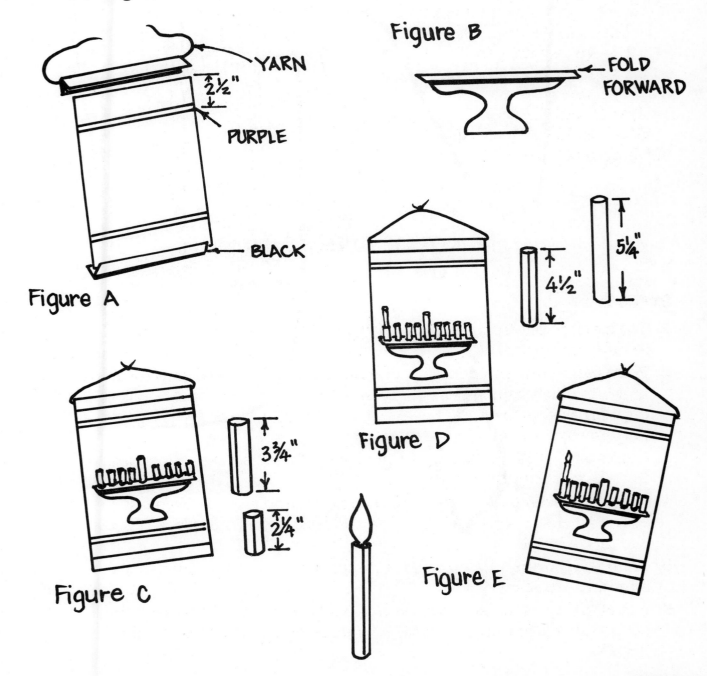

Figure A

Figure B

Figure C

Figure D

Figure E

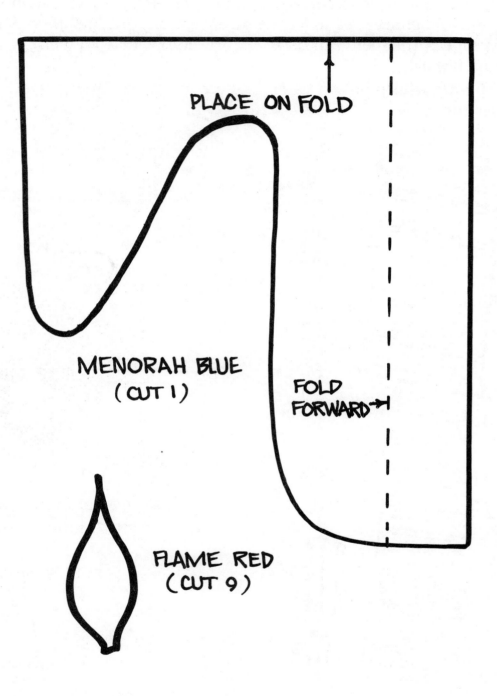

PLACE ON FOLD

MENORAH BLUE
(CUT 1)

FOLD
FORWARD

FLAME RED
(CUT 9)

Aluminum Foil Mask

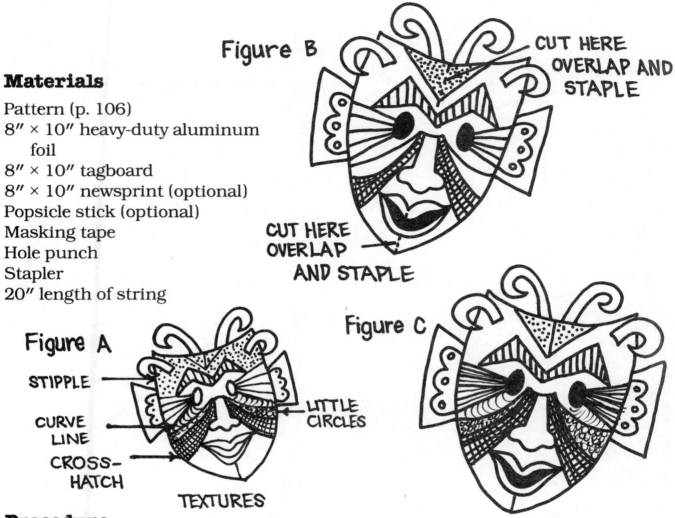

Figure B

CUT HERE OVERLAP AND STAPLE

CUT HERE OVERLAP AND STAPLE

Figure A

STIPPLE

CURVE LINE

CROSS-HATCH

LITTLE CIRCLES

TEXTURES

Figure C

Materials

Pattern (p. 106)
8″ × 10″ heavy-duty aluminum foil
8″ × 10″ tagboard
8″ × 10″ newsprint (optional)
Popsicle stick (optional)
Masking tape
Hole punch
Stapler
20″ length of string

Procedure

1. Apply glue to entire surface of tagboard. Cover with aluminum foil.
2. Tape mask pattern (or your own design drawn on newsprint) over aluminum foil.
3. While glue is still wet, trace over design with a dull pencil. This will transfer design to foil. Allow to dry.
4. Remove pattern and cut out foil mask.
5. Create texture on mask with pencil or popsicle stick (fig. A).
6. Cut out other details from foil scraps to further decorate mask. Staple in place (fig. A).
7. Cut in 1½″ at top and bottom of mask. Overlap cut edges and staple together to create a 3-D effect (figs. B and C).
8. Punch one hole on each side of mask. Thread string through and knot ends. Mask may now be worn.

Holiday Gifts and Decorations, © 1986

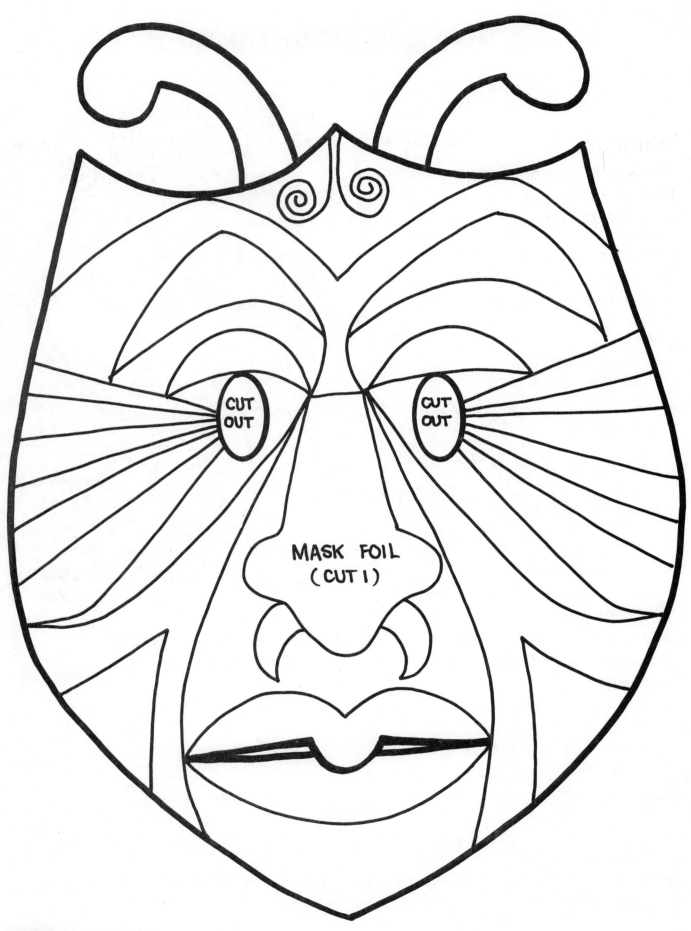

CUT
OUT

CUT
OUT

MASK FOIL
(CUT 1)

Jar Lid Ornament

Materials

Two-piece canning jar lid
5″ × 8″ art paper of any color
   (background)
Greeting card
6″ length of yarn
2″ × 2″ cardboard
Tagboard scrap (hanger)

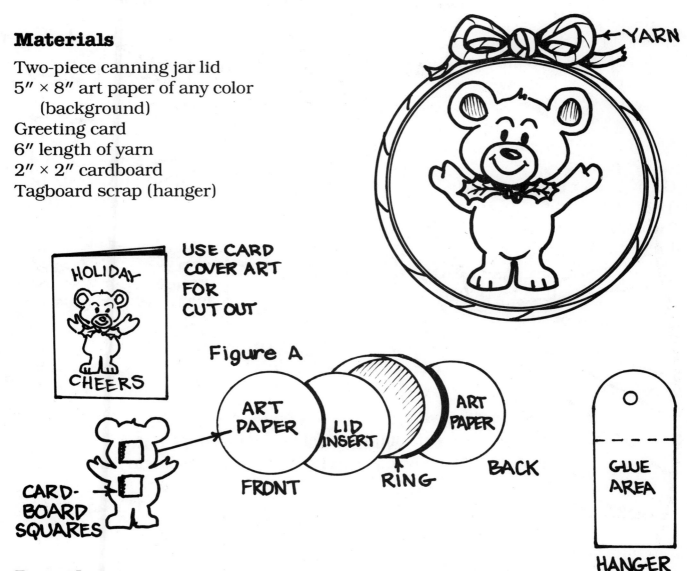

Procedure

1. Trace lid insert on art paper and cut out two circles.

2. Glue lid insert to inside of lid ring (fig. A).

3. Glue paper circles to inside and back of lid (fig. A).

4. Cut figure(s) from greeting card.

5. Glue ½″ cardboard squares behind greeting card cutout(s). Glue cut-out(s) to front of ornament (fig. A).

6. Tie a yarn bow around top of ornament for decoration and hanging.

Note: If this is to be a wall hanging rather than a tree ornament, trace hanger pattern on tagboard, cut out, and glue to back of jar lid.

Holiday Gifts and Decorations, © 1986

Shoe Box Treasure Chest

Materials

Patterns (this page)
3½″ × 11″ red art paper
Gold or silver metallic paper:
    two 1½″ × 13¼″
    two 1½″ × 10″
    6″ × 12″
Scraps of red, green, and black
    art paper
Green poster paint and brush
Two 12″ lengths of red yarn
Two brass fasteners
Hole punch

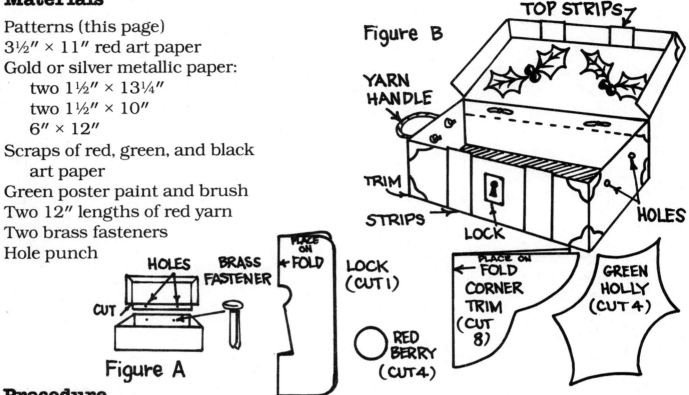

Procedure

1. Paint a shoe box and lid with green poster paint. Allow to dry.
2. Cut two corners on long side of lid and fold back for hinge (fig. A).
3. Punch two holes in back of box and in hinge so brass fasteners can join lid to box (fig. A).
4. Punch two holes at each end of box about 1″ from top edges. Thread yarn through holes and tie for handles (fig. B).
5. Glue two 1½″ × 13¼″ strips of metallic paper around bottom of box (fig. B).
6. Glue two 1½″ × 10″ strips of metallic paper around lid. Glue ends of paper under front and back lid edges (fig. B).
7. Attach lid to box with two brass fasteners (fig. B).
8. Trace and cut out corner trim from metallic paper. Glue in place (fig. B).
9. Trace and cut out lock from black paper. Glue lock to 1¼″ × 1¼″ piece of metallic paper. Glue lock to box as shown (fig. B). Trace and cut out other details.
10. With black felt pen, write greeting on red paper. Glue cutouts in place on inside of lid.